Family Memories

PHOTOS
ALBUMS
JOURNALS

Suzanne McNeill & *Lani Stiles*

Photography by David & Donna Thomason

Design Originals, Publisher

*"To All the Memories of
Our Family and Friends."*

Many Thanks to our wonderful family...
Lois, Trey, Kelley, Todd, Steven, Kristy,
Margaret, Dale, Wesley, Dustin, Ashley,
Liz, Leizl, Brendy, Kelly, Leisha, Greg,
Carley, Rose, Alex, Taylor, Katy and a
Special Thanks to our friends... Donna,
David, Patty, Janet, Kathy, Linda, Jean,
Virginia, Laura, Barbara, Julie, Delores,
Kim, Kyle, James and everyone else who
took photos, posed, shared memories and
helped make this book possible.

A Beautiful 'How-To' Book
Copyright ©1996 Design Originals
by Suzanne McNeill and Lani Stiles

Published by **Design Originals**
2425 Cullen Street
Fort Worth, Texas 76107

Library of Congress Catalog
Card Number: 96-85256
McNeill, Suzanne.
Stiles, Lani.
  Photo Memory Albums handbook - 'How-to'
capture the best of your family photos and memories
in keepsake albums / Suzanne McNeill.and Lani Stiles
   1. Photos 2. Albums 3. Journals 4. Genealogy
5. Crafts 6. 'How-to' Source book I. Title

CIP
UPC   23863-05005
ISBN   1-57421-005-X
10 9 8 7 6 5 4 3 2 1
First Edition - Printed in U.S.A.

Family Memories

Opening an age old box of photos is like lifting the lid of a treasure box. Each picture carries a valuable story of its own. When we see it, the event is instantly replayed in memory. Unfortunately, most pictures are buried in boxes and stacked behind a closet door. Prized possessions such as photographs are meant to be seen and enjoyed. Long ago, a family album of black and white portraits was kept to document the family tree, but today albums remind us of many occasions. From family albums to personal journals, spaces abound to display the hundreds of photos most of us store in dusty old shoeboxes.

Photos mean so much more when we can share the pictures, the heartfelt stories and the memories with family and friends.

"A picture is worth a thousand words...with a story, it is worth a million more."

Our first **Family Memory Album** was organized when several overflowing shoeboxes tumbled into sight. Picking up pictures one by one brought to mind stories about the colorful images. Inquiries of who, where and when began to pop out. We both ended up learning facts and hidden secrets about the people and events in the photographs. At first it was fun and games trying to remember. Then as we dug deeper into the pile we couldn't recall which year it was, who was in the background or where the pictures were taken. Counting candles on the birthday cakes, studying faces in the background with a magnifying glass and guessing at the holiday by the color and theme of the decorations became our only clues to what the stories behind the photos were all about. It was a day which turned into a late night and ended in discovery, ultimately inspiring us to revive, record and rediscover the story of our lives.

After finding the photos it seemed a waste to allow the memories to be tucked away and not seen. The shots of the family together at Thanksgiving this year would soon be joining the shots from last year behind a dark dormant closet door. Of course our family photos started in one of Mom's kitchen drawers close enough to be reviewed during holidays, but over the years the collection grew into a shoebox and now at least twenty years of special occasions occupy six cardboard boxes with no rhyme or reason.

So, we decided to get started ... and the following is what we discovered, learned and created.

Suzanne and *Lani*

Contents

"Families who share many happy memories stay together."

Lois Browne

"Shared memories leave footprints in our hearts."

Family Ties

For families, looking through photos is a valuable exercise for sharing memories. By communicating thoughts and feelings about the events captured on film family members learn about each other. Like a history lesson, the importance of people and dates is passed on to younger generations. It is a lesson of values and family heritage which can only be taught at home.

Create a family album with your children. Interview grandparents, aunts, uncles, cousins, family and friends. Insights into family choices and how lifestyles evolved are documented in the lives before us. We have so much to learn about ourselves. Pictures and stories bring understanding to situations we are faced with throughout life.

Start organizing photos in the room you share with your family after dinner. Encourage everyone to pick up a few pictures and start telling stories Ask them to write down what they remember. Place their handwritten recollections directly in the album with the photos. You will have an archive with original handwriting to keep and treasure for years to come.

Treasured Family Memories

Nestled in drawers, treasured photographs, mementos and notes are hidden from view. Although they are one of the most precious possessions we save throughout the years, days go by with no attention to their sentimental worth. If not carefully stored in archival quality boxes and albums, photographs are in danger of deterioration. In addition, the memory which is attached to each captured image is in danger of being lost or forgotten.

Surrounding ourselves with keepsakes and memories of happy times is invaluable; not only for adults but for children too. Given a set of photos, children have the opportunity to learn family history.

By displaying family pictures in the home, a kindred presence of relatives fills every room. Moreover, a Family Memory Album is the perfect place to organize a box of pictures and a mind filled with memories.

"Family memories create a chain of love linking the past with the future."

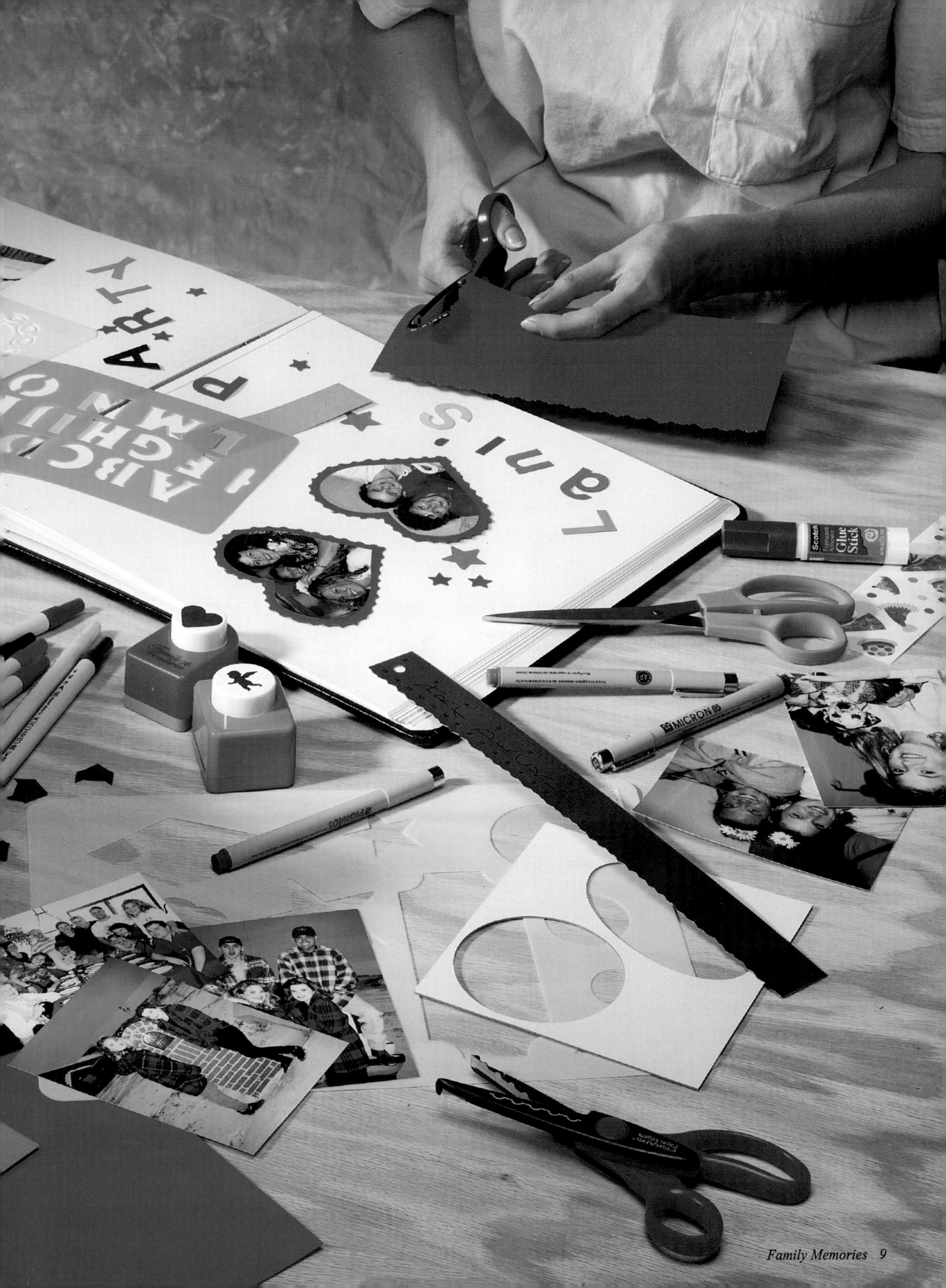
PARTY
Lani's
Scotch
Glue Stick
MICRON 05

Quick letters - Stencils colored with marking pens make lettering perfect every time.

Great look - Use wavy scissors to cut off corners of photos then mount on colored paper.

Double color - Cut two 'look-good-together' colors of paper for great photo mats.

Sticker Fun - Add colorful stickers as accents and borders for photos and pages.

Organize and Choose

As soon as a roll of film is developed, I can't wait to pull open the flap and be the first to see how all the pictures turned out. Some shots are great, some set the scene and others should be hidden from sight. The immediate impulse is to organize these photos into a story to share. Without doubt, there are mementos and expressions of the moment which add to the pictures. Capture all the best to make a treasured Family Memory Album.

To get started, gather all the pictures you plan to organize in one place. A work space or table that you can leave undisturbed for a period of time and room enough to spread out photos and divide into themed events is ideal. To ensure that no unnecessary dust, dirt or oil from your skin transfers to photos, wash your hands before handling photographs. Wear light cotton gloves for extra protection.

Sort and edit photos by choosing the absolute best shots; the ones with expression in the faces, ones of the whole group... you know, the ones which make you smile and bring back the moment as soon as you lay eyes on them. Good photo images display expression, emotion, texture... you'll want to capture it all. Compare clarity and sharpness of the images. Identify emotion, action, color, faces, gestures, shadows, close-ups and details. Select an order, whether chronological or thematic, for your album. Estimate a two-page spread. I usually choose 8-12 photos for each event in the album. The easiest times to remember are the ones that just occurred. I suggest that you start with the most recent set of pictures and work backward.

Photo borders - Draw decorative borders around photos with colored markers.

Highlight a photo - Silhouette a special picture by cutting around the primary figures.

Line up pictures - Line up your photos and space them evenly to show order.

Highlight a picture - Cut a photo in a special shape (a heart, a balloon, a star) to add interest.

Effective color - Use wavy edge scissors to cut background mats of colored paper for photos.

Angle photos - Angle your pictures in an arrangement and overlap them to create groupings.

Add color - Use an entire sheet of colored paper behind pictures for a colorful page.

Journals - Don't forget to 'Tell the Story' by writing a brief description of each event.

Draw attention - Highlight a good photo by cutting it in a round or oval shape.

Tip...Easy lettering - Use rubber stamp alphabet letters to add titles and headings.

Titles are important - Use markers and decorative lettering to 'Tell the Story' at a glance.

Basic Tip! Cut most pictures in basic rectangles... save unusual shapes for special photos.

Arrange Photos

Page arrangement will depend on the shapes and sizes of photos and keepsakes. A combination of large and small images surrounded with headlines and words creates a great deal of interest for the eye. After selecting which photos you want to include on a page, experiment, arrange and rearrange the images until the grouping pleases you.

Allow for space to add mementos and to journal. Accent photos by pulling out the theme with keepsakes, ticket stubs, lettering, calligraphy, colored markers, a ribbon, thumb prints, clip art or writing. Journal around photos with narrative such as names, dates, location, stories, quotes, feelings, poems, history or thoughts. It's all relevant and important. Self-expression, your unique keepsakes and memories are what make any album special. After choosing the photos and keepsakes for a page, arrange them in logical order. If your photos are too large, crop around the image to leave space on the page for colorful mats, words and keepsakes. Next, layout and mount the photos one-by-one using photo corners, adhesives and tapes. Finally, write a brief description or story to remember the events portrayed by your pictures and mementos.

Special photos - Draw attention with a paper star.

Add interest - Line up pictures and overlap them in an arrangement to add order.

Silhouette - Cut around the actual figure in a photo then mount it on colored paper.

Add color - Punch motifs out of colored paper to add sparkle and design to pages.

Add accents - Use strips of colored paper...either as borders or to highlight photos.

age 6

Baby Kristy 'Our little STAR'...

School Days

Brother Todd

Little League

Kristy M.

with Brothers

Friend Amy

Friend Carley

Sister Kelley + Caterpillar

Mom Suzanne

age 10

Sister Lani

Grows Up ~1...16

Brother Steven

Kristy... still a STAR! 'Sweet 16'

Cropping

While arranging photos you may recognize unnecessary blank space around the subjects which can be omitted. Cropping strengthens a photograph by focusing attention on the subject of the picture and cutting away unwanted background or distracting images. Since cropping alters the photograph, experiment by using two corners of paper to form a 'window' to cover sections of a photo before actually cutting.

It is easy to get a clean cut edge with a mini-trimmer, scissors, or an X-acto knife and cutting mat. In addition to cutting a photograph, cropping can also done at the time the photo is taken. When looking through a camera's viewfinder, narrow the focus to the image by standing a little closer to the subject or using a zoom lens to get a better view.

When taking pictures of people, get to an eye level position. The subject can then interact with the camera making the photos more intimate. Memories are best reflected in people's faces where expression and emotion can be captured.

A single photo may be cropped several different ways. In this photo, the subjects were surrounded by distracting items in the background. Simple centering and off-centering with 'square' shapes make the subjects more important.

"The best and most valuable things cannot be seen or even touched... they are fond memories that must be felt with your heart."

Creative Cropping

Center template over photo then draw around it. Cut the shape out with scissors.

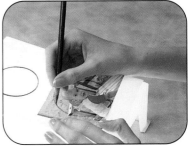

Optional: Center a photo over a paper template on a light table. Trace, then cut it out.

Another creative method of cropping is the use of decorative shapes, edges and page themes. Cutting shapes and mats for photographs draws interest in and around the image.

Photo templates are guides for cutting circles, ovals, rectangles, octagons and more. The best templates are made from translucent plastic so you can see through the template for accurate centering. For homemade templates, try using cookie cutters, kitchen glasses and bowls as guides.

Scissors with wavy edges can be used to cut photos, photo mats and colored paper.

Journals

The Story... *finding the right words depends on the theme of an album. Words can be few or many, poetic or casual. Although photographs display an image, descriptive narration of the who's, why's, where's and how's help tell the story. Who are all the people in the background and how do they relate? Where was the picture taken? Outside or inside? On what occasion? Pictures are the visual...a few words can turn subjects into family, friends, neighbors or strangers. Dates of photos also give reference to places and events. Seek out details and be descriptive when writing the narrative.*

Writing can be brief to include a simple caption under each photo. To do the least amount of writing possible, simply label your photos with basic information. Dedicate the first page of your album to a chart with columns to include the most pertinent information, such as date, event and order number of the photographs. To add more information, write a short sentence to bullet points. An entire paragraph with as many details as you can recall will give more depth to the story.

Handwritten notes are personal expressions both from the writer and for the recipient. Children write wonderful notes. They say what they think without thinking first, so open and honest with expression. What can be a protected or embarrassing sentiment for an adult may come freely from a child.

Personal handwriting is part of the memory and part of you. Have others write in the album as a memory to them and of them.

"The more descriptive the journal, the more complete the memory will be for generations to come."

Kristy
and Carley
AGE 15
ANTIGUA GUATEMALA

Over Spring
Break my
mother, aunt,
cousin and
grandmother
went on a
Guatemala, We shoppe[d]
[C]hicastenango, visite[d]
[A]titilan and enjoyed
[s]eeing in Antigua a[nd]
[Guate]mala City. When
cute photo-hor[se]
[ha]d to have my p[icture]
to commemora[te]
my mom too[k]
[pictu]re in Mexi[co]
Kristy

Slumber Party

Let's
stay up
all nite
- - -

Linda and Virginia took the sl[umber]
Party to its literal meaning. Showing [up]
with night gowns, curlers, house shoe[s]
and sleeping bags was a surprise to al[l]
the other guests. They didn't take ov[er]
for an answer when trying to recruit
others to dress for the occasion. Suzanne
was taken under their wing and decked
out in all her finest. She dressed in
a favorite sleeping gown adorned with
snowmen and pink pigs. The gown
must have been a gift. Everyone
knows Suzanne has a vast collection
of pigs including kitchen towels and
salt and pepper shakers.

I was lucky enough
to get away before being
recruited into the dress.
After posing with those [pigs], I made a

Golden Girls
When I moved to Dallas,
Texas in 1931, I was in high school. Some of my best friends from school are still my best

friends today... Mimi, Jane,
Margaret, Mary Jane,

Dot and Nita. Now in
1996, we are about
80 years old and our
granddaughters are
in highschool. Lois Browne

Born to Be Wild

Basic Tools

The most important tools are probably ones you already own... like scissors, a ruler, adhesive glue or tape and a pen. Although these items will be enough to get started, a few additional tools are available that will make working with photos easier and faster.

While sharp scissors are adequate for straight cuts, consider an X-Acto craft knife with a replaceable blade for clean cuts and easy handling. To save the blade of the knife and prevent cutting into your work surface, use a self-healing cutting mat. Another cutting tool is the mini-trimmer. It is a miniature paper cutter, perfectly sized for cutting 3"x 5", 4"x 6" and 5"x 7" photos.

Glues and adhesives vary in application, permanence and photo-safe quality. Glue sticks are non-toxic, acid-free and readily available. Glue line dispensers, double-stick tape and photo splits are simple to use. Check to see that glues and rubber cements are archival quality and acid free so they will be safe for photos.

Colored markers with brush tips and writing tips and colored paper help make pages and events memorable.

Rulers keep cutting edges straight for photos, mats and colored paper. Also use rulers to lightly pencil in guidelines for journals.

Wavy edge scissors and decorative punches are fun to use. Templates are the greatest find to improve photos. Look for oval, circle, star, hexagon and heart shapes. See thru templates work best to crop unwanted background away from the subject. Cookie cutters come in great shapes and are easy to trace around when used as templates for teddy bears, hearts, fish, circle and juvenile shapes.

Use a double-stick 'tape line' dispenser to make 'lines of tape' to attach photographs and colored paper to pages. Note: Additional photo adhesives include glue sticks, double-stick tape and rubber cement. Use white glue and tacky glue to attach braid, small pieces and momentos.

Use an X-acto craft knife, a cutting mat and a ruler to cut photos and colored paper. Measure and line up photos or paper with the lines on the mat. Change blades in the knife to keep them sharp. Note: It is also simple to cut around silhouette photos with an X-acto knife and mat.

The mini-trimmer is one of my favorite tools. Use a mini-trimmer to cut photos quickly. Line each photo up on the lines so they will be square. For perfect cuts, pull the handle slightly toward the center of the cutter and hold the photo steady as you cut.

Colored Paper

Paper is the essential component of which a photo album is constructed, as well as being the most basic and decorative of embellishments between photographs and the blank page. The specific qualities of the paper you choose will vary in weight, strength, texture, color, coating and fiber properties.

The weight of paper affects its flexibility. Heavyweight paper is sturdy and is best used as a base for more delicate papers. Lightweight paper is easily folded, cut, torn and scored for use as photo frames, deckle edged mats or cut paper designs. Textured paper is thick or thin, soft or hard, matte or glossy. The neutral colors of handmade papers are often accented by herbs and natural grasses to add to its texture.

Japanese papers are light, absorbent and contain long fibers. Tissue and crepe papers come in pastel and bold colors, patterned and even transparent. Card stock is often protected by a foil-covered or glossy coat which retards some paints, markers and pens. Common construction paper provides an assortment of primary colors ideal for children's projects. Resume papers in light pastels with little texture are available from stationery stores. Gift wraps are invaluable for adding design, pattern and color interest to an album page.

Paper contains varying degrees of acid from its natural chemical makeup. Although acid can eat away or yellow photographic images, many papers available in art stores are acid-free for safe archival use.

Throughout this book, different papers have been used in the album pages. It is worthwhile investing in an array of papers so that you can experiment with textures and colors that add to your album.

Make a colored paper mat for a special photo.

"The love in our family leaves memories for us to treasure and

Tear or cut out decorative strips and shapes to create colorful memory albums.

Create colorful double mats to draw attention to special events and photos.

Be clever...
cut out mats
for photos to
highlight special
memories.

Tear or cut shapes
out of colored
paper to highlight
an event or theme.

Use wavy scissors
to cut decorative
strips and shapes
of colored paper.

Make a colored
paper mat for a
photo with wavy
scissor edges.

Punch out colorful
shapes to decorate
pages of your
photo album.

Be creative! Add
color and dimension
to album pages.

Cut colored paper
into decorative
shapes for mats.

Brush tip marking pens make vivid colors for 'Bubble letters' and for drawing borders.

Write, add decorative borders and journal on black album pages with easy-to-use metallic silver and gold markers.

Use flat tip Calligraphy point marking pens to create elegant letters. Practice, practice... writing beautiful words with calligraphy tips is simple once you get the knack.

Colorful Pigma® pens have acid free characteristics, Pigma ink is fadeproof and waterproof.

Copy clip art on pages 98-103. Color images with colored pencils then cut around shapes to use for album decorations.

Use stencils with Pigma® or fine tip markers. Outline letters then fill in with brush tip markers.

Markers

Event titles, photo labels and journaling are immensely important to memory albums. They increase the value of every story and memory. Lettering for page titles and photo descriptions is essential to any good album page and can easily be beautiful and decorative with the help of markers, pens and colored pencils. With a little practice anyone can master attractive penmanship with the following tools.

Colored pencils are the most basic. Using a pencil is like using the pencil you learned to write with in grade school. Colored pencils are best to write a paragraph, color a clip-art outline or color around a photo.

Paint markers come in a rainbow of vibrant colors. Like using a pencil, a marker sits comfortably in the hand. When the color flows through the soft tip, a stream of brilliant hues are absorbed into the paper. For more options, look for markers with dual felt tips. One end creates a fine line for outlining and lettering, while the other marks a thick line for bold lettering and coloring.

Easy-to-use markers in metallic gold and silver are also available. They are especially valuable tools to write on black album pages. They may also be used to add decorative lines, borders and writing.

Another decorative tool is a calligraphy marker. Calligraphy markers have a flat felt tip to 'automatically' angle your penmanship. A few practice strokes are important to get comfortable with the attributes of this marker.

For purely archival albums where special care is taken to use only acid-free papers and materials, Pigma® pens are invaluable. When used on acid-free pages, Pigma® pens take on acid-free characteristics. In addition, Pigma® ink is fadeproof and waterproof. Colors, fine tips, medium tips and calligraphy tips are available.

"The memories shared between generations...from grandparents to grandchildren are priceless."

Use punches on a sturdy surface or table. Place punch flat on surface then press evenly and hard.

Punch small decorative confetti shapes, bears, trees, hearts, stars, etc. with hand-held punches.

Use a corner punch to round the edges of a photo or mat, or use a rounded template and scissors.

Punches & Scissors

Two innovative tools designed to add motifs and customized edges to paper are decorative hole punches and wavy edge scissors.

Punches have familiar punch out designs...ovals, hearts and stars to unique shapes like teddy bears, cats, dinosaurs, sailboats, trains and palm trees. After punching a shape from colored paper, use it in your photo album as confetti, as a mat arranged symmetrically around a photo or as a border to outline a page of photos. Punches can be used to create confetti punch out shapes or the paper can become a decorative frame surrounding an album page or photo.

Wavy scissors are edged with scallops, zigzags, ripples and other shapes to cut paper. Try cutting photograph edges, photo mats from colored paper, shapes, lettering and paper strips to weave. The ideas and possibilities are limitless. After cutting a piece of colored paper with scissors, notice that one side of the cut has an opposite shape from it's counterpart.

Both punch motifs and scissor designs are reversible.

Wavy edge scissors make great borders for photos, mats, colored areas and colored strips.

Try turning wavy edge scissors upside down to cut paper...the design will usually be different.

Line up wavy edge scissors carefully to make a symmetrical line as you cut each row or shape.

Rubber Stamps

Rubber stamping only requires one stamp to make several designs. To ink a rubber stamp use either an ink pad or rubber stamp markers to mark on the stamp itself. After applying ink from the pad or marker carefully lay stamp on paper and press firmly without rocking the stamp. With one stamp a whole page can be decorated by repeating the design in a border pattern. The stamp design can be an outline of an image or can be colored in with markers for a bold image. Stamping is a creative way for children and adults to embellish a page of photos.

Use ink pads in a variety of colors to decorate pages.

Brush tip markers may be used as ink with stamps.

Color different areas of a stamp with brush markers.

Stickers

Colorful stickers are fun and easy to use. They may be purchased in a variety of colors, shapes and sizes. Simply peel each sticker off its backing then place it any-where you like on an album page. Stickers are permanent and some are acid-free.

Peel each sticker off of the backing then place it on the page.

"The most treasured heirlooms are sweet memories of our family and friends."

Stencils

Add terrific designs... alphabet letters, borders and frames...to paper in a colorful manner with stencils. Stenciling is a way to reproduce an image with a minimum of effort.

Stenciling is a simple method using paint or markers. To make your own stencil cut a card or acetate to make a design. Purchase reusable stencil designs from a craft store.

To create an image on the surface underneath a stencil, apply color through the stencil leaving an image underneath. Markers, pencils and pens can be used to outline and color in a stencil.

When coloring, it is important to hold a stencil firmly in position with removable tape to ensure the image does not shift while working with the colored markers.

Use border design for pages.

Stencil frames around photos.

Stencil alphabet letters to make titles for pages.

Photo Albums

Photo albums, just like books, come in different sizes and formats, including the manner of binding. To choose the best album you will have to rely on your individual preference. Consider whether or not the album will be archival to protect photos for a number of years, whether your album will be displayed on a living room book shelf or whether the album will need to lay perfectly flat for display. Archival albums have acid-free and lignin free papers for the ultimate in preservation quality. To be sure, read the labels or ask a photo shop for assistance in locating these albums. Note: Archival albums may have black or white pages for display and may have parchment dividers between each page to further protect the photographs from dust, dirt and natural chemical reactions. If your album will be on display or standing on a bookshelf, it is important to choose a sturdy covered album. In addition to withstanding constant handling, a strong binding and structure will maintain its form while standing on a shelf. Albums which stand, as opposed to lying on their side, act as a preventative against deterioration caused by the possible chemical reactions between photographic papers. Album bindings differ greatly; it is worth consideration before making a purchase. Ring binder albums allow for adding, deleting and reordering of pages. Bound albums have spines that resemble hard cover books. Fine covers of leather or linen offer high quality display in a formal library book shelf. Post-bound albums hold punched pages together with metal posts. Scrapbooks are usually oversized for enlarged photos, documents and souvenirs. With such roomy pages, they also make great albums for journals, photo stories and keepsakes. Journals offer ample space to record personal reflections but the spine has to be broken in order to lay flat. If an album gets too bulky with keepsakes, clip out every other page to allow more room. An expandable spine can be adjusted for any number of photos or keepsakes.

"I'm just as lucky as can be...for the world's best memories belong to my family, my friends and me."

Expandable Spine Albums

Expandable spine albums allow for any number of photos.

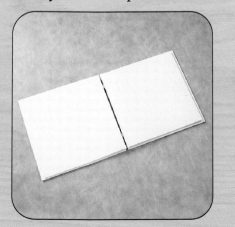

Expandable spine albums lay flat and pages can be rearranged.

Spiral & Ring Bound Albums

Spiral bound albums expand but the pages are difficult to rearrange.

Ring bound albums expand and the pages are easy to rearrange.

Journals & Post Bound Albums

Journals and book bound albums work well for bookshelves.

Post bound scrapbooks are large and the pages can be rearranged.

Friends are the Flowers
in the Garden of Life

Felt Covered Albums

Blanket Stitch around the edges.

Felt Album Covers - 1. Open an album flat, lay it on felt then cut around the album adding 1/4" to all sides. 2. Decorate the front area of the album with felt flowers, stitching and buttons. 3. Open the album. Cut two fabric panels 1/4" larger than the inside covers on all sides. 4. Iron HeatnBond™ to the back of the felt cover and panels. 5. Lay fabric over the album then iron fabric to cover. Use the edge of a ruler to press fabric into the hinge near the spine. 6. Close album then iron fabric to the spine and back cover. 7. Iron panels to the inside covers. 8. Use 4-ply embroidery floss to Blanket Stitch around the album.

Fabric Covered Albums

Iron fabric to the front of album. Open the album then miter each corner by cutting it at an angle.

Fold each corner and iron. Next fold the side to the inside. Iron all edges to the inside of album.

Album Covers - 1. Iron HeatnBond™ to the back of 1/2 yard of fabric. 2. Open an album flat, lay it on fabric then cut around the album adding 2" to all sides. 3. Lay fabric over the album then iron fabric to cover. Use the edge of a ruler to press fabric into the hinge near the spine. 4. Close album then iron fabric to the spine and back cover. 5. Open the album. 6. Miter corners leaving just enough fabric to overlap. 7. Wrap fabric around then iron to inside cover. Repeat for back cover. 8. Slit fabric at spine, turn inside, attach with white glue. 9. To line inside covers, cut two fabric panels 1/2" larger than the inside cover on all sides. 10. Fold and iron a 3/4" hem around fabric panels. 11. Iron HeatnBond® to each panel then iron to the inside cover. **Photo Frame Covers -** Optional: 12. Cut fabric 1/2" larger than mat. Cut quilt batting to the same size as a cardboard mat. 13. Iron fabric to batting. Iron HeatnBond® to the back of batting. 14. Iron to the front of mat. 15. Miter corners, fold edges to the inside then iron in place. Add a photo then glue to album.

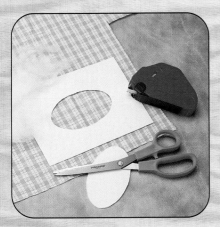

Cut batting the same size as mat. Cut fabric 1/2" larger than mat.

Fold and iron fabric around the mat. Glue to the front of album.

"Many years from now, it will not matter what I had, where I went or when. What will really matter is the memories of family and friends."

Shared Memories

Traditionally photo albums and scrapbooks provide a place for 'Show and Tell', while journals and diaries give a place for recollection and sentiments. Family Memory Albums are full of stories and we are the storytellers.

Albums and journals are personal displays. They usually contain information relating to the style and intent of the 'albumeer' including photos, words and mementos. Few books are more personal or more lasting.

A phrase that I love, "there is nothing better than sitting down with a good book" is also true of sitting down with a collection of photos, stories and memories of my family, friends and home.

Brandy-Carley

Kelley-Steven-Trey-(maxwell)

1996-Brothers + Sisters Todd-Kristy-Kelley Steven-Trey + Iani

When I asked Mom about the first Family Memory Album, she remembered an incredible fascination with a collection of photos of her parents, Nanny and Smokey. Smokey, named because he was always smoking a cigar or a pipe, probably shared the photos with Mom while Nanny was in the kitchen cooking dinner.

Nanny loved cooking gourmet food and the kitchen was her domain. Her other favorite room was the adjoining formal den where she kept the carpet perfectly vacuumed, so much so that you could always see the parallel lines the vacuum cleaner left as she went from side to side in perfect measure. It almost appeared as a fresh mown lawn with a pattern across the surface. We are not sure if she kept it freshly vacuumed for guests attending her frequent tea parties or just to make sure no little children walked into that room full of breakable antiques. One step on the dense yellow carpet left an irreversible impression of shoes right down to the signature indention of the soles.

Mom remembers Smokey sharing the photo album and describing the pictures. He was the tall one sporting a mustache and dressed in the army uniform. During World War II, he was stationed outside of Rome, Italy. When he returned home, it was the first time he laid eyes on his baby girl.

Now that Smokey has passed on, the photos are important links to the past. For Mom, memories of sitting on Smokey's lap and hearing his stories are even more cherished. The thought brings tears to her eyes and the photos joy to her heart.

SUNSHINE DAYS...
1979-1995
JENNIE & DAVID

OUTING AT THE RANCH
TEXAS STYLE

Memories, Friends & Happy Hours

Sunshine Days - Looking back through the years of collected photos, Julie chose Sunshine Days as a title to remember her children growing from infancy to young adults. It is amazing how quickly children change through the years, while adults seem to stay just the same. Yellow construction paper was cut into a semi-circle with extending rays to create a brilliant shining sun.

Outing at the Ranch - Candid photographs capture unexpected moments. Just when you thought no one was looking, a friend appears out of nowhere and clicks a few photos. Surprise!

Our Family - All year long we look forward to a family reunion at Thanksgiving. We look forward to gathering at my sister's home in the Texas hill country. After a big turkey meal everyone appears to have commemorative family photos taken...first Nanny and her girls, then Nanny with eight grandchildren, next each family and finally individual photos. These photos are our treasures.

Fire - Gathering to begin rebuilding a lost home was a happy ending remembered with the help of bright orange colored paper and sunflower stickers.

Home - A group of friends gathered to help the newlyweds celebrate the completion of their new home. The rub-on decal picturing a house set in a country field added to the event as the party was captured in the photos.

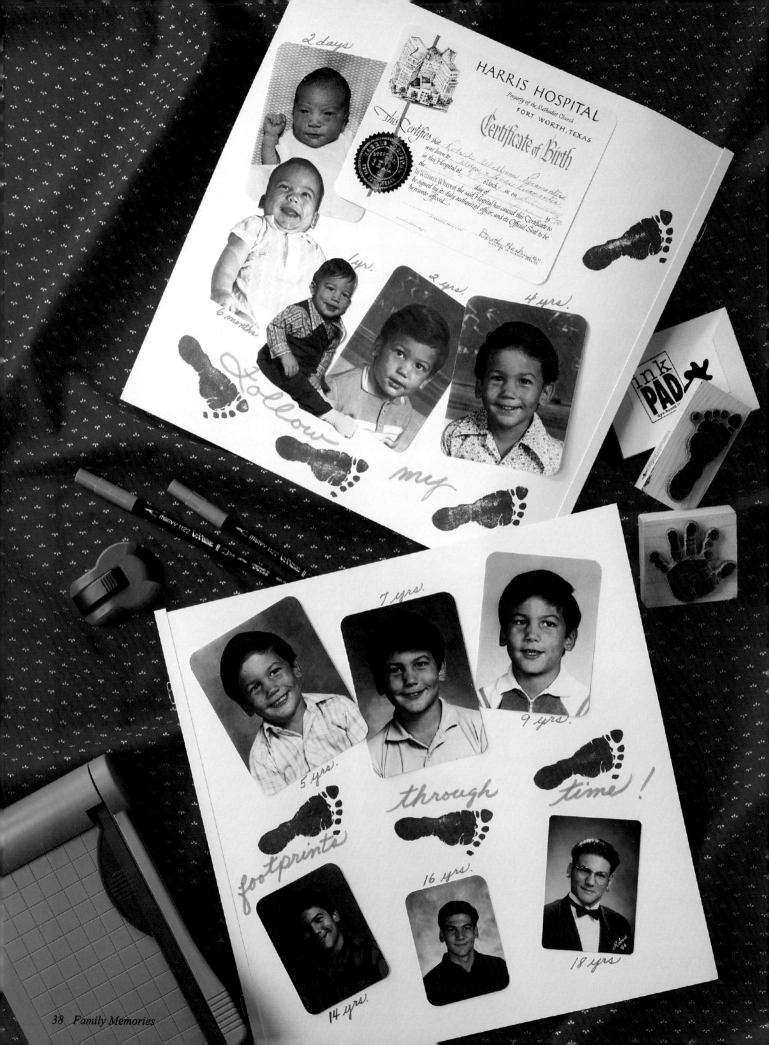

Mothers Understand What a Child Does Not Say

Follow my Footprints - School photos from kindergarten through college follow Robert's changes from year to year. Each step of the way is stamped like a footprint across the page.

David and Jennifer - As each child sits behind the wheel of their first car and drives away on their own, it seems like only yesterday when they were just born and held in a protective mother's arms guarding against the dangers in life. A boy's page and a girl's colorful page are personalized by blue and pink paper mats placed behind the collection of photos.

Memory to Jonann - She gave so much love and left us with many precious memories. These pages speak the photographic language of love and reflect love for one who was only beginning to blossom. Jonann stayed only a little while, but left us with a lifetime of memories to be cherished. A heart marked with incremental ages heads the ribbon and bow framed portraits.

Sleepy Time Guy - Some photos speak for themselves. Snapped in the wink of an eye and treasured for a lifetime. Each picture inspires endearing memories. A favorite is Brad's chubby little legs poking from his crib. One could fall under the spell of a storyteller imagining how these circumstances might have happened.

Friends Forever

Best Friends - Kristy and Amy saved a collection of photos from grade school lunch hours to high school proms. As a birthday gift, Kristy arranged and decorated the photos for Amy. Of all her 'Sweet Sixteen' gifts, Amy claimed this was her favorite.

Happy Days - Long time friends join to celebrate the birthday party of a very special person. Photos of the cake, the gifts, the friends, a birthday card and all the memories fill these album pages..."Happy Birthday to Suzanne".

Great Food, Good Fun - At this famous rib joint in Chicago, a friend thought it would be fun to bring along a camera to the celebration. Now the whole gang is remembered for wearing bibs and eating with barbeque-covered fingers.

Entertaining - When Jim and Pam come to visit from California, we always get together to enjoy conviviality, funny jokes, original food and the remembrance of good times. The hostess captured all her guests on film, a night to remember and friends to cherish.

"Warm hearts are nourished by fond memories of family and friends."

Precious Pets

Mother and Daughter - A love for horses runs in the family. Although these photos were taken generations apart, mother and daughter find the same interests.

Dog Bones - Paw prints made from a rubber stamp look almost real as they make a border around the page. Delores treats her chow dog like a prince. She even made a paper dog house for Sugar.

Dalmatian Puppies - Ribbon and paper designs can be found in most craft and card shops. Stickers, a greeting card and playful puppy ribbon, all picturing dalmatian puppies, accent this group of photos.

A House without a Cat is not a Home - Who says cats don't pose for pictures? Everyone in the family posed for this page and Muffin is on center stage.

A Show Horse - No ordinary horse, Mary Lou competes for the blue ribbon. Here she is joined by fellow equine stickers.

My Dog Morgan - A dog is man's best friend but a puppy is a young girl's best friend. Stamps of running puppy paws make this page colorful.

"Fond memories are always close to my heart."

SCHOOL DAZE

Terrific!

Rose Kilber

Wimberley, Texas

Excellent!

My favorite teacher was Miss Robins in the 4th grade.

1+1=2
Aa Bb
Cc

School Days with Miss Rob
about Egypt and Africa
class Guinea Pig (Katy)
Guppy fish have babies
a carnival for Hallowe

SCHOOL

• 1994 •

include learning
caring for our
watching our
every year we have
where everyone
comes in costume,
even the teachers.
One year my
mom came as
a witch with
long black
hair. As
we got
older,

we
became
better
friends
as we
cheered
on our
boys in
football
and on
to Senior
Activities and
Graduation.

VOLLEYBALL

Sports are an important activity
for Kristy. A good athlete committed
to improving her volleyball game,
Kristy was so proud to make
an outstanding spike against
a fierce competitor. Martin.
Kristy was the outside hitter
on the first string volleyball
team for Crowley Eagles during
her sophomore year in high school.
Purple and white just happen
to be her favorite colors this year.
Cheerleading was also among
Kristy's after school activities. I
often wondered how she kept up
her grades. She is an all around
talented girl, not to mention

School & Kids

At the age of 13, I made my first photo album with the inspiration and leadership of my Spanish teacher. Every year Mrs. Deneen invited a small group of students to experience not only Spanish as a language but as an adventure on a chaperoned trip to Mexico City and the ancient pyramids. For months prior to the journey, she taught students about the country of Mexico. Before the trip, each student was to organize and title a binder containing pages for each day of the journey. An itinerary for the day's sights and excursions included suggested photos for the album.

I kept a travel journal and saved mementos of ticket stubs, postcards and little treasures marking the path of the adventure. From that first album, I learned the importance of the story to be told by an album. The photographs and mementos became clues and significant additions to the narrative, and so, I became a writer, a storyteller, a historian, an editor and a photographer for one of the most memorable experiences of my life.

Often teachers and coaches take a special interest in the development of their students. This is a perfect opportunity to make a commemorative album. With the guidance of an instructor the album becomes a learning tool. Whether the book marks the milestones from one year in school and sports or marks the particular accomplishments of each student who passes through a particular program, it is a collection of memories unmatched by any other learning tool available to teachers, coaches and students.

A yellow school bus and red schoolhouse are classic reminders of learning, children and school days...symbols of timeless images.

School Awards

High School - Bits of fading memorabilia and mementos serve as personal reminders of the way we were...the senior prom, Friday night football, special friends. Keepsakes from school days highlight award ceremonies, special honors and a date to the prom.

Grade School Memories - Souvenirs of childhood days which all too quickly slip away. Photos strengthen our identity and record the landmarks of our life. Take a deep breath my son and "Live for today, but remember the past." Grade school memories, a kindergarten diploma and favorite cards represent the treasured possessions of a proud mom.

Brad Bowling - Bowling was serious business when Brad stepped up to the lanes. His bowling form was good enough to be featured in both the morning and evening editions of the newspaper.

Go Team Go! - When letter jackets wear out, precious patches are mementos to be saved. Flat enough to lay in a scrapbook and be joined by an award certificate and team photos.

College Graduation - Photos provide a visual record of the milestones of our lives. Years of planning, expectations and scholastic accomplishments were realized on graduation day, "Well done, son! You did it in four years!"

Magical Moments

Track and Field - Track pictures of Trent are a delight to see. The fun and excitement of his sixth grade track competition bring back the joy of raising a son. Pictures in this album also remind Trent of his friends and family from high school days. "If only we could extend happy times with our children." Brightly hued paper cut in the shape of a first place ribbon adorns the page of track and field photos. Yellow, pink and blue mats were cut slightly larger than the photos of tug-of-war and relay races.

Pee-wee to Varsity - Memorable years highlight Junior's way from pee-wee to varsity. A series of chronological photos which show his advances from pee-wee to varsity football is complemented on the opposite page with a newspaper headline, team picture and symbol of the school mascot.

Cheerleading Team Competition - While oversize photos of the team picture all the cheerleaders in action, a silhouette version of Kristy shows a jump she practiced for months. Days leading up to the competition were full of excitement and anxiety but nothing matched the intense emotions of each participant.

Homecoming - A first date! Laura's first homecoming...a day to be remembered. The homecoming corsage with streaming green and gold ribbons dresses this album page in the school colors. Bold letters traced from a stencil and cut with an X-Acto craft knife spread across both album pages.

Graduation - Virginia is the proud mom celebrating the accomplishments of her daughter, Tanya, on these three pages. Mother, father, grandparents, brothers and friends were there all along reaching out with support and encouragement to move forward. An added blessing to the moment was the youngest family member, Haley!

HOMECOMING

WHHS

Not only was Homecoming '92 my first Homecoming, it was also the school's 25th anniversary! Lots of Hills alumni came to watch the game, including my best friend's parents, who were Class of '73 graduates. The Cougars beat our long-time rival, Paschal high school, 14-3.

MING 92

My first high school date was my freshman year Homecoming. It was exciting! Mom managed to get a photo just as we left for the dance. I felt so grown-up.

My date and I, all dressed up for the Homecoming dance!

CHS - 93

Tanya and her little blessing made it through a senior year with the love from their family.

DADDY'S Pride

Hey Mom! We did it! HALEY

Brother's LOVE

We like a hand in a glove!

EAGLES

MOM'S JOY

LET'S CELEBRATE

Mrs. B's star students

Terri
Tim
Jake
MRS. BURNETT

Daniel
Jabe
Jeff

SoA

SCHOOL

This year has been my favorite. I love to read, to visit the zoo and learn about animals. Taylor

Sports and baseball are my favorite part of school. I also love history. Josh

My dad is an engineer and I want to be one too. I love trucks and cars and love to assemble things. Alex

YEARS

Being a model or actress is what I want to do. In school Theatre Arts is my favorite class. I also love horses and loved going to the FFA, Future Farmers of America convention in Kansas City. Kristy

I plan to play professional football after college. Am working very hard to keep my grades up and be a good team player. I hope to get a scholarship to pay for college.

Teach Them Well... Children Are Our Future

Mrs. B.'s Star Students - Star shapes in rainbow colors fill the background and highlight pictures of this teacher's star students. A paper punch was used to make the small stars while the big star mats were traced from a template.

Student Messages - Mrs. B. asked each student for a small class photo. Next she asked each child to write a short message about their favorite school activity. Each year Mrs. B. adds to her collection of valuable students...she is sure that each one will become important.

Yearly Journal - A year to year summary of the events of a class of students and their activities. Not only is it a memoir of the teacher's career, but of the school and the students she has helped over the years.

Field Day - A proud teacher insists on highlighting "students of the year." Everyone can get involved with ribbons, stickers and journal memories.

Powder Puff Football - Cut from brown and white paper, the football captures the event celebrated in pictures. Even more fun are the conversational bubbles above the participants.

Teachers and Students - A rubber stamp alphabet produced these quirky letters in blue ink. Use a plastic template to make cutting photos in octagonal shapes a breeze. Crop each photograph, then adhere it to colorful paper. Finally trim with wavy edge scissors.

Christmas DAY

This year we celebrated the Christmas holiday at Suzanne's house ... 3 whole days filled with baking cookies, pies, and cakes...

Steven, Kristy & Todd

Suzanne

Kelley   Kristy

Sug & Kristy   Liz

Steven   Trey

Todd

Taylor   Dale & Lane

Kristy   Kelley   Lois

Todd   Baby Katy

Kelley & Steven   Kristy & Suzanne

Suzanne Todd

making little cards and special gifts ... wrapping presents ... visiting with everyone young and old. And on Christmas Eve we went to the candle light service then ate dinner. A very special time for ALL.

Todd

Steven

Although holidays come but once a year, they are remembered all year through as a time when family members gather to celebrate. Even if we cannot be with family, we think of them and remember childhood holiday times together.

Whether the occasion is a national holiday, a religious celebration or a reunion, the event is monumental enough to leave fond thoughts in memory. In addition to thoughts, mementos give hints as to the sights, sounds and smells of the occasion. Pictures remind us of the importance of family, of times spent together and of the love and support that is always available.

Thanksgiving is one gathering you don't want to miss in my family and yet, I am unable to travel from New York to Texas for every holiday of the year. My mom takes a picture, usually a whole roll, of all the important stuff, like the turkey, the cranberry sauce, the honored guests who get to take a chance at the previous year's wishbone pull, the old guys playing 'bridge', the young guys playing 'hearts' and the little ones playing 'go-fish'. From the roll Mom picks one great picture to adorn the front of the card which everyone has taken the time to sign, "Wish you were here".

The thought, the photo and the inscription of signatures is the next best thing to being there. All the cards and photos are now saved in my valuable Thanksgiving album.

Christmas Cheer

What Did You Get for Christmas? Santa brings all kinds of surprises and this year the surprises were caught on film, even the morning 'want-to-stay-in-bed head'. Cropping out unnecessary background highlights the subjects of good photographs. Facial expressions and personalities permeate in the pictures and in the candid words Kim remembered from her family.

Christmas 1995 - Everyone's favorite reindeer hangs photos of friends and family from his antlers. Creatively cut balloon shape mats from a template make ball ornament shapes large enough to hold round snapshots. Cranberry red and evergreen mats in the shape of Christmas balls are reminders of Christmas holidays spent at Grandma's house.

Holiday Ornaments - A string of ornaments dangles with colorful stickers across the top border of these pages. Memorable photos of friends and neighbors decorating ceramic ornaments at a painting party portray the festive atmosphere of young and old alike.

Celebrate the Holiday Season - Holiday gatherings are opportune events to capture all your friends with smiles on their faces. David and Donna's yearly extravagant celebration is famous for good food, homemade eggnog and conviviality. Photos with double mats using festive shades of crimson red and kelly green complete the scene.

Christmas at Grandma's - Our family celebrates Christmas for days before the official date. Everyone arrives with a recipe for cookies, candy and pie to make at her home. One year Aunt Suzanne had been to Australia where pumpkin is considered an everyday vegetable so she made pumpkin soup, pumpkin pancakes, pumpkin bread and baked pumpkin. Festive ribbon and poinsettia stickers fill in nooks and crannies between the photos.

A Fine Spring Day

Spring Flowers - Visions of spring are best remembered in blooming flowers and a back porch birdhouse. Both are cut from bold patterns and filled with faces from the picnics in the country.

Easter Memories - Remember when children were small by saving pictures with special holidays characters.

Baby Faces - Sweet little baby faces are doted on by parents and grandparents alike. Not a moment to forget when they grow up so fast. Here the precious photos have text to tell the story behind the scene.

Memorable Portraits - Posing for photos with the Easter Bunny, Santa Claus and Mickey Mouse, childhood characters of the imagination, fills the air with celebration during holiday seasons.

Happy Easter - Kids decorate bunny baskets with yellow, pink and green eggs and grass. Easter baskets in hand, children dressed in their best dresses and trousers fill these pages.

Happy

a

Nanny, Keisha, Rosie, Carley, Brendy, Kristy

To make Easter special, everyone decorates eggs.

Todd and

Easter

Decorated eggs, the "Hunt" and family photos of everyone.

Kelly, Todd and Alex

Alex and Rosie love eggs

Kristy McNeill + Rose

Rosie and Steven...tied up

Fun in the Pumpkin Patch!

For Danny's first Halloween, Dad was in Italy, so Mom took pictures of us to send.

We bought lots of pumpkins and played with them in the yard. Danny got excited and pulled at my hair and knocked Jeff to the ground. We all wound up in a pile on the grass, rolling around laughing while Mom got frustrated 'cause we wouldn't hold still for her to get good pictures.

Finally, we got some good photos and then we got to carve the pumpkins and cook the seeds to eat. Jeff's pumpkin had lots of teeth, but mine had two missing in the front 'cause I did too. Danny had a pumpkin too, but he couldn't draw the face or carve it out 'cause he's too little, so we helped him with his.

The Great Pumpkin Caper

Danny crawls through the pumpkins in our backyard.

What's this? I wonder what's inside....

Boo-who! Pumpkins are scary!!!

Mom finally get us to hold still and pose for a good photo to send to Dad.

Laura & Barbara

Halloween, Thanksgiving, New Years & Valentines

Fun in the Pumpkin Patch - Celebrate childhood joys...choosing and decorating pumpkins. For this page Laura and Jean designed funky letters to set the mood in the Pumpkin Patch. Lettering styles abound since the boom of home computers. Notice the decorative letters used in magazines, look in your library for typeset books or create your own personal lettering style to use as page headings.

Halloween - Pumpkins galore...a greeting card, a few pumpkin stickers and favorite photos of the annual fund raiser, the pumpkin painting party. Good friends and clever pumpkins are forever remembered in the photos taken at the event.

Thanksgiving - Although holidays and pictures of the family go hand in hand, it is the memories that remain special from year to year. Looking back on pictures of last year's Thanksgiving dinner reminds

us of the golden turkey, Grandmother's homemade cranberry sauce and pecan pies. Remember to write in the family journal. The memories, the recipes and the events tell a story to be enjoyed by anyone looking through the family album.

New Year 1996 - What was your New Year's Resolution? Enjoy family and friends then commit your resolution to paper.

Valentine's Day - This special anniversary page is full of heartfelt ideas to symbolize the Valentine shape. Red paper, a pair of painted lips, lots of hearts and a pretty bow tell the tale.

"Hearts are filled with fond memories of family and

LEISHA

1996

BRENDY (MOM) + LEISHA

BRENDY and CARLEY

ALMOST READY... CARLEY, LEISHA and ROSIE,

LEISHA'S DRESS STILL FITS!

MARRIES

What a Happy Day! Leisha planned her own wedding... chape[l] cake, flowers, dres[s] reception and food[.] It was perfect! Leisha was the m[ost] excited bride i[n]

GREG GIBBS

"Wishing You Only Happiness Together FOREVER."

The Chapel... in Downtown DALLAS

The BARNETTE-LEISHA... A BEAUTIFUL BRIDE.
-KILBER FAMILY...
Kelly-Carley-
Leisha-Alex-Rosie-Brendy.

Let Gregg carry You!

"Going Awa[y]..."

Wedding, Baby & Birthday

When I worked in downtown Boston, it seemed our entire department was getting married or having babies. We were in a non-stop parade of showers. A gift for each occasion became overwhelming until we started giving little gifts of experience. For a wedding shower, we all got together for an hors d' oeuvre party and each person filled out a recipe card for the newlyweds. For job promotions, we presented albums full of photos, quotes and unforgettable stories.

Instead of buying a gift, make an album. Included below are a few more ideas.

Baby's Book - For posterity, the pages in a baby album collect, record and display the start of new history. Safely store baby's first words, first photos and first memories in a special album. Someday they will want to know.

Children - Young hearts are full of emotions and questions. "Where did I come from? Who brought me into this world?" As a gesture of support and care, make an album of all you know about a child. Someday they will want to know.

Birthday Book - For a 40th Birthday we sang "You're a Good Fellow" and made up words about forty years of friends. Everyone was commissioned to bring a picture of a humorous event, a family outing and a forgotten moment. Later all were combined into an album with photos from the party itself.

DEBBIE'S WEDDING

The wedding and reception was held in the middle of Lake Granbury on the "Granbury Queen" riverboat. Debbie and Jim spend many long hours handmaking the invitations.

The bride wanted a small casual wedding so the bridal party and families wore western style clothing. Debbie looked beautiful in her tea length dress and white boots. She made her hair decorations and arranged all the flowers herself. Cindy Fortune made a beautiful tiered cake that was delicious. She missed the ceremony on the upper deck because she stayed on the lower deck making sure that the movement of the boat would not make the cake topple over.

Debbie's good friend, Laurie, was maid of honor and John, Jim's brother was best man. Of course Edwin (Dad) gave away the bride. You could just see the love on his face. Timmy was the one and only usher and the all young girls wanted to know if he was single. I promised that I would not cry, but I did.

The Captain of the riverboat married Jim and Debbie and the crew served a great meal. We all enjoyed ourselves and wished that the cruise had been longer.

Debbie and Jimmy
September 18, 1993

Deborah Alleen Frantz
and
James Wayne White
invite you to share our happiness as
we exchange wedding vows in an
informal ceremony Saturday,
September 18, 1993, aboard the
riverboat "The Grandbury Queen".
The party begins at 4:30 pm when
we leave the dock for a 1½ hour
cruise. Casual attire is
appropriate and jeans and boots
are welcomed. Please accept
or decline by September 12, 1993
with enclosed card. Reception
following ceremony.

#31 Delores Frantz

Weddings

Debbie's Wedding - Mementos of the ceremony and wedding day surround the page with vivid memories. The invitation and a personalized souvenir napkin are reminiscent of the day's intent and style. A story of the entire day of events was written on the computer to allow for space. The beautiful type was chosen for its elegance. Simplicity invites you to read about that day.

A Dream Come True - A dreamy white wedding complete with ribbons and pearls to have and to hold for always. From handmade paper, a corner is adorned with dried flowers set in the textures of the paper.

Remember When - Old and new come together to celebrate 50 years where an antique wedding announcement lays opposite the photographs of the couple recreating their vows 50 years later. To complement the colors of the announcement, cream and moss green papers were cut in strips with wavy edge scissors and layered side by side.

A Garden Wedding - Any roll of pictures is worth remembering, here a home garden wedding is captured by an amateur photographer. Although the photos were taken many years ago, the memory of the moment is still alive. While stenciled flowers and hearts border the page, a careful hand mixes colored markers to border around individual photos and bold markers recreate the day.

Nancy's Precious Moments - For a large portrait and white invitation, try choosing a delicate paper doily for the border. By cutting out the center of a placemat size doily there is enough room to display the entire invitation and angelic portrait of the young bride.
Note: A careful hand spliced the doily to size and small scissors cut within the doily design.

"Shared memories
are the golden thread
that tie hearts together."

For Danny's second birthday, I made a big Cookie Monster cake, Since he was Danny's favorite character on Sesame Street. When he saw the cake, Danny got really excited and ran around the house yelling "C is for cookie! Cookies are for me! I want cookies!"

Once we finally calmed him down, we put him in his chair with the cake in front of him. Danny stared straight down at the cake and threw his whole face into the frosting! What a mess!

Once we'd cleaned him up, we lit the candles and sang Happy Birthday. We told Danny he was supposed to blow the candles out, but he was too captivated by the fire (a young pyromaniac?). The candle wax dripped all over the cake and we had to blow the candles out instead.

After I'd scraped the waxy part of the frosting off, we cut slices and served the cake. When we put Danny's plate before him, he stared at the cake, not sure what to do. Then he messily ate some and sat back up...not quite sure if he liked the cake or not.

The **B**irthday **b**oy

Hello?

Just a minute...

...it's for you, Mom (probably a salesperson)!

Laura A. Kievlan

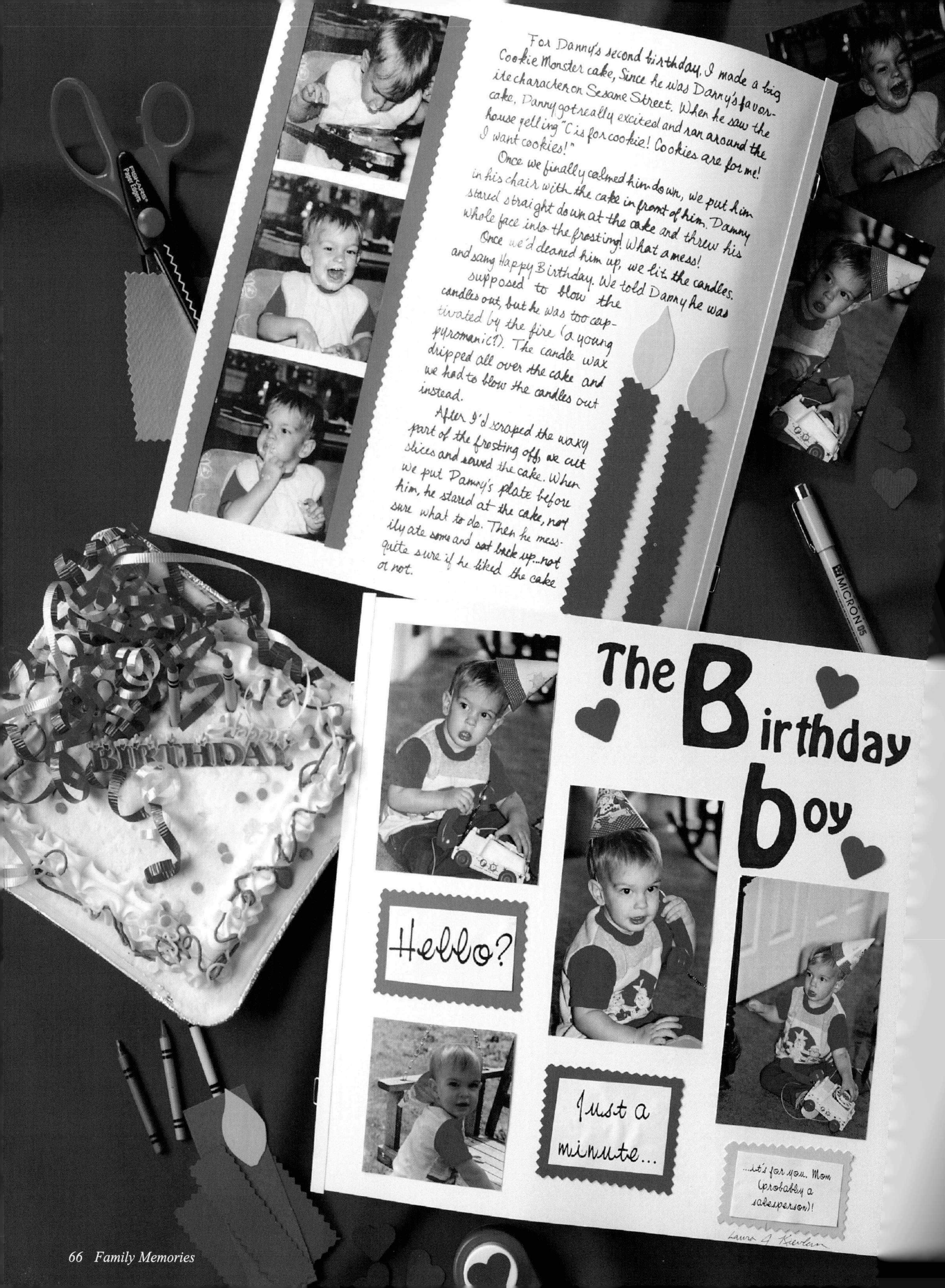

For Danny's second birthday, I made a big Cookie Monster cake, since he was Danny's favorite character on Sesame Street. When he saw the cake, Danny got really excited and ran around the house yelling "C is for cookie! Cookies are for me! I want cookies!"

Once we finally calmed him down, we put him in his chair with the cake in front of him. Danny stared straight down at the cake and threw his whole face into the frosting! What a mess!

Once we'd cleaned him up, we lit the candles and sang Happy Birthday. We told Danny he was supposed to blow the candles out, but he was too captivated by the fire (a young pyromaniac?). The candle wax dripped all over the cake and we had to blow the candles out instead.

After I'd scraped the waxy part of the frosting off, we cut slices and served the cake. When we put Danny's plate before him, he stared at the cake, not sure what to do. Then he messily ate some and sat back up...not quite sure if he liked the cake or not.

Hello?

The **B**irthday **b**oy

Just a minute...

...it's for you, Mom (probably a salesperson)!

Laura A. Kirvan

Weddings

Debbie's Wedding - Mementos of the ceremony and wedding day surround the page with vivid memories. The invitation and a personalized souvenir napkin are reminiscent of the day's intent and style. A story of the entire day of events was written on the computer to allow for space. The beautiful type was chosen for its elegance. Simplicity invites you to read about that day.

A Dream Come True - A dreamy white wedding complete with ribbons and pearls to have and to hold for always. From handmade paper, a corner is adorned with dried flowers set in the textures of the paper.

Remember When - Old and new come together to celebrate 50 years where an antique wedding announcement lays opposite the photographs of the couple recreating their vows 50 years later. To complement the colors of the announcement, cream and moss green papers were cut in strips with wavy edge scissors and layered side by side.

A Garden Wedding - Any roll of pictures is worth remembering, here a home garden wedding is captured by an amateur photographer. Although the photos were taken many years ago, the memory of the moment is still alive. While stenciled flowers and hearts border the page, a careful hand mixes colored markers to border around individual photos and bold markers recreate the day.

Nancy's Precious Moments - For a large portrait and white invitation, try choosing a delicate paper doily for the border. By cutting out the center of a placemat size doily there is enough room to display the entire invitation and angelic portrait of the young bride.
Note: A careful hand spliced the doily to size and small scissors cut within the doily design.

"Shared memories
are the golden thread
that tie hearts together."

Baby Books

MeMe's Haley - Stepping stones are big for baby even when Grandma is there to help. At only 3 years of age a page full of memories from the fiRst day to first words. A special memory is a photograph of the first day of baking cookies together.

Thank Heaven for Little Blessings - A second baby is just as important as the first. Pictures of Trey, Liz, Taylor and the whole family celebrating the new arrival of Katy are surrounded by a ribbon from the shower.

Artist in Training - Only a photo can capture a special moment in time. Santa knew an easel would make this little budding artist happy on Christmas morning. When the artwork is taken down from the refrigerator door, a protective album is the perfect way to preserve it for years to come.

Mother and Daughter - Rummaging through a box of black and white photos revealed an unlikely find. A 50 year old photo of a baby girl that almost exactly matched another photo taken over 35 years later of that girl's daughter. Nearly identical down to the face, hair and beautiful smile.

Grammy's Little Angels - Linda says, "If I had known grandchildren would be so much fun, I would have had more children." Her grandbabies are so special that she framed them in unique mats made from stickers, stencils, paper and markers.

"Encourage children to see pictures and hear stories of your childhood. They love knowing that you were little once, just like them."

Birthday Wishes for Every Year

The Birthday Boy - Beyond the photographs, journaling tells a story. "For Danny's second birthday, I made a big Cookie Monster cake . . ." Although the pictures only show the birthday boy, the journal tells about the person who makes the album. Jean baked and decorated a creative cake with her son's favorite character from Sesame Street.

Happy Birthday Party - This page and the party for Roger come alive by simply placing colorful lettering, balloons and confetti stickers around the photos. Since everyone signed the birthday card, placing it on this page is a reminder of all who came to celebrate.

You Take the Cake - A bold red, white and blue theme complete with stars and a little flag creatively pull out the image in the photograph. Upon opening a big box, Todd uncovers a rugby shirt in the colors and design of the American flag.

Just 50 Years Young- For this surprise birthday party Jeanette decorated with black to symbolize "Bill is over the Hill at just 50 years!" By cropping photographs in rectangle, oval and square shapes more images fit on the page.

"Happy memories are secrets of the heart."

VACATION TIME

Each Spring my year she chose a 'Girls Only' trip to our teenage girls— went to Antigua, Attilan, Guatemala. Every day was visited, shopped, seeing with the We all in the bright the beautiful hand-carved wooden angels and animals. Most of all we love gentle and beautiful indigenous and peoples. Children are especially friendly and especially loved talking with Carley and Kristy. Guatemala is truely a magical place.

Carley-Lois-Suzanne-Kristy
Browne McNeill

GUATEMALA

Fantastic!

sist...
any pla...
visit Guatemal...
Carley (17) and K...
Panajachel, San...
City and Chichicasten...
special as we
went sight—
and talked
Mayan Indians
markets.
loved
colors,
huipils,
and
the

BRAVO! her on

I MISS YOU ALL!

LAND OF ETERNAL SPRING.

JUST DO IT!

Shopping

SUPER!

Our Parisian Adventure

Sacre-Coeur Basilica

Ile Saint Louis

Montmartre

Le Louvre

Beaubourg

Cathédrale Notre Dame

Tour Eiffel

Jardin des Tuileries

This page of my album is just like going back to Paris for David and me. We spent 10 exciting days, including our 13th anniversary, exploring and soaking up Paris and it's perimeter. I recall all the sounds, smells and sights and all the places in between from the photographs. I just can't take enough photos in such beautiful, romantic and historic places.

For my husband and me, our personal photo albums are just like a book written about our life together...the people we love and the memories we share.

Composition, subject and the order of pictures communicate our story. With the stories and pictures, we add a photo essay. By simply arranging the photos in chronological order and underlining them with a brief caption, our photo journal tells a story on its own.

Travel and vacation albums and journals are the perfect place to record a story in the making. With a small notebook, we jot down brief notes to remember each day and we often make rough sketches of favorite locations. We take lots and lots of photos. Later we transfer these notations and combine our favorite memories with photographs to create the story of the trip.

CAMP

fun DaYS

EL TESORO 1995 · BUDDIES · FRIEND'S · Counselors in Training

My mother went to camp El Tesoro when she was 8 years old... and I went when I was 8 years old. El Tesoro has given me so many fond memories... my friend Toni and my 1st horse, my good times. From camper to...

Counselors in Training. Let's have fun.

Counselor! Kristy 1995

Kristy - C.I.T. 1995.

Counselors - Kristy - Toni

Toni has been my friend since I was 8 years old... 1987. Kristy

Campers and Counselors. It is just soooo HOT.

Campers round the flag.

Kristy & HOT.

E.T.

FUN AND

Rosie and Alex

Chloe

Allie and Beverly

Amy-Emily

Summer is a really special people and hang-out with friends. to go to camp, on vacation, This summer I went to camp songs, swimming,

BEST FRIENDS

Chloe and Molly

Heather and son

Emily and Amy

Emily

Trey and Todd

Josh

With no School, I get time to play with friends. visit special people and hang-out with friends, camp for a month... horseback riding, games, food and fellowship. My Best Friends have a special place in my HEART!

Camp & Summer Fun

Camp - Journaling intertwines with photos to remember Camp El Tesoro friends and summer fun. Every year from the second grade to high school, Kristy has enjoyed the same camp her mother attended when she was a schoolgirl. Framed in red and blue, the group photo names all who appear in candid moments captured by individual photos.

Fun and Best Friends - Bright bubble balloon shapes cut with the aid of a template make perfect mats for photos of friends. A few words written at the bottom of the page remember the event.

Indy 'Miata' - A trip to the Indy 500 race track in Indianapolis was inspired by a new car. "How do we get there? Where is it? What is it?" Make an album with a child to remember a trip. Learn geography by using a map to plan the route and destination.

NASA - Blast off to NASA! Danny posed with the astronauts while Mom snapped photos. Then Mom chose a headshot to glue into the astronaut lineup pictured in the brochures. Mementos saved from a journey become part of the memory album page.

Wet and Wild Days - Fun in the sun all comes back with pictures of Slip 'n Slide in the front yard under the old oak tree. Young boys make every day special on summer vacation from school.

Horses - This horse has a real home complete with fenced in corral and red barn. Alternating bubble letters repeat the color scheme chosen for the background. Trotting in and around the page are cropped photos and equestrian stickers.

Vacation Fun

Sunny Sailing - Fun in the sun in the summertime is beautifully illustrated with the creative use of shape and color. By creatively cropping photos in the shape of triangles and umbrella tops, the photos themselves become design tools in the sunny scene.

At the Beach - Happy frogs help hold down photos of Barbara's day at the beach. Plenty of sand and surf will tell the story as the photos are used full size with little cropping. Titles and stickers add interest to the page.

Flying - All the details of Kim's vacation to Mackinaw Island are pictured in a glance from photos, a map and her husband's flying airplanes. Reading the caption in the red box only makes the story better.

Sand and Shore - Footsteps in the sand reveal the most amazing finds. By looking through a magnifying glass, seashells were found buried on the shore. Dolphins were spotted in the surf. Each photo is strategically laid on a portion of map with blue water to mat it and the looking glass frames the exact location of the beach.

4th of July - With a folk art flair, pictures of the Independence Day are remembered here. Star shapes cut from felt fall between photos. Journaling describes the occasion.

"Few things in the world are treasured like happy memories."

POSSUM KINGDOM LAKE

Fishing With Grandad!

Reeling in the "BIG" one

Catch of the day!

FISHING TRIP 1995

Our weekend was filled with FUN, SUN, and FISH. Hopefully, we are going to make this an annual event with our cousins.

"Catch of the Day"

The one that got away...

Nap time?

Look at this guy.

PORT ARANSAS

At it again!

Nice Catch!

Kodak

MICRON 05

Terrific Trips to Remember

Fishing with Granddad - Pictures of children with their grandfather are a reminder of all the fun times they have had fishing with him. On this afternoon Raymond had his hands full. The rustic cabin at Possum Kingdom Lake still brings back loving memories of unexpected moments.

Deep Sea Fishing 1995 - Bigger than life is Kelley's fish story. Although the bottom border shows most of the fish that got away and stayed in the sea, the photos show a few BIG catches of the day. Wavy edge scissors cut colorful construction paper mats for the photos and one picture postcard.

Traveling West - Virginia and T.R. trace their journey from East to West... from Niagara Falls to the Grand Canyon this couple remember the wonderful travels and cherished moments. A simple page title and blue cloud wrapping paper tell the story and make this page attractive.

Angling Days - "What's tugging on the line? " asked Edwin. "The Big One... a 12 pound black bass to win the fishing competition is on the end of my line," exclaimed Delores.

Colorado School Days - "My Mom took every opportunity to visit me at the University of Colorado to share a day in the mountains," said Lani.

Grand Adventure - After a 10 day rock and roll raft trip down the Grand Canyon and a 10 mile hike into the canyon, Bob organized a reunion party to share the video he made of the adventure. Everyone exchanged snapshots to relive the stories.

Backpacking *in Colorado*

One of my favorite trips...we River Rafted in Pilar, visited Santa Fe, and the Chama Valley in New Mexico then on to Colorado - 1995.

Camping in the Snow,

Governor's Palace,

Wanda

Keri and Suzanne ...real Outdoors women.

Smile! Hi! OOPS!

The train station in Chama,

Smile!

Independence

4th of July Parade...Lake City

Is my tent really water proof? OOPS!

Memorable Moments

Backpacking in Colorado - Backpacking in bold letters tells the story. Ten days with five wonderful friends formed bonds that will remain with us forever. We rafted the Pilar River and visited the Chama Valley in New Mexico. Then we drove on to Lake City and the Rocky Mountains in Colorado.

The Get-Away - A favorite cabin in the woods and memorable days fishing celebrate the joys of life. A colored paper border is cut with wavy edge scissors to set page boundaries. Within the border, patterned leaves fall in fabric prints of plaids and stripes.

Autumn Leaves - The fiery, brilliant colors of Autumn leaves come and go with the season, but here, naturally dried and pressed, the leaves hold their color to remember this fall day in the park.

Fun at Disney Land - Kids and adults alike enjoy Disney adventures. On this trip, the Kievlans took photographs of their children with costumed characters.

Whether a few photos or many, mats draw attention to the individual images. By using different colors of paper and a variety of wavy edge scissors, each frame is unique.

"Part of the fun of doing things is to share the memories with family and friends."

GUATE

During Spring Break Kristy-Suzanne-Carley-Nanny-Brendy went to the land of eternal Spring... Guatemala.

McNeills-Brown-Kilber

Friendship

♥ More Bracelets

Horseback

MALA 1995

Carley + Kristy

UNITED STATES

MEXICO

GUATEMALA · BELIZE
HONDURAS
EL SALVADOR · NICARAGUA
COSTA RICA
PANAMA

Where is it? Why would you want to go there?

Beautiful Huipil

Still Shopping

The Last Night

GUATEMA

...a living Mayan museum

Guatemala is a magic place.

Kristy-Nanny-Carley

Two of Kristy's New Friends.

Our little Van... full of ethnic treasures.

Carley-Kristy and Friends

LA 1995

Kristy + Carley play flutes.

View from our hotel.

3 Generations... Suzanne Nanny Brendy Carley and Kristy.

We learn about the Mayan shrine... Popal Vuer

Exotic Trips to Foreign Lands

A Living Museum - A visit to Guatemala is like stepping back in time hundreds of years...native weavings, colorful 'animales' figures, Mayan ceremonies and ethnic people who live and dress as they did centuries ago. These photos highlight a day at the market in the ancient town of Chichicastenango. The exact location of Guatemala is pinpointed on a hand traced map of Central America.

Guatemala - Every year Brendy and I take our mother on a special trip...away from family and everyday responsibilities. The trip pictured here included our teenage daughters for a week in Guatemala during Spring Break. Everyone practiced Spanish and collected Friendship Bracelets.

Ecuador - Photos of exotic travel to foreign lands can often fill an entire photo album with markets, ethnic people and native traditions. Lani organized pictures and memories of a trip to South America in magazine style. By cropping photos into rectangles she was able to add journaling on colored paper.

Amazonia - As Suzanne watched a T.V. special on Amazonia, she never dreamed she would visit there. Traveling down the Aqua Rio, she saw tapirs, fresh water dolphin, piranha, colorful birds, wild monkeys as they floated down miles and miles of water.

The Animal Market - Each Saturday hundreds of animals are brought to an acre outside the village. Squealing pigs, patient oxen, sheep, chickens and cattle fill the air with smells and sounds. People barter and sell until new owners lead the animals away.

DANCERS WEAR
COLORFUL COSTUMES
OF THE VARIOUS
REGIONS.

THE MEN PLAY
IMPORTANT ROLE
IN DANCES.

DEMONSTRATION OF
DANCE TO CELEBRATE THE
FESTIVAL OF THE
PINEAPPLE HARVEST.

TICKET TO MUSEUM
IN MEXICO CITY

AIRLINE TICKET
TO OUR OAXACAN
ADVENTURE!

SUZANNE & ALL
HER COLORFUL LITTLE
FRIENDS.

MEXICO CITY
AIRPORT - THE
EXCITEMENT IS
MOUNTING!

WE'RE OFF!

SUZ SAMPLING FRUIT
AT VENDER STAND.

The Magic of Mexico

Aztec adventures - Textiles and handwork seen in country villages inspired bright designs and photo mats from a trip to Oaxaca, Mexico. Linda cut Aztec-inspired borders for the pages. Linda kept every memento along the journey, an airline ticket and travel receipts, to glue on the page for authenticity.

Oaxaca - Many shapes and sizes of photos create a festive feeling to celebrate this trip to the highlands of Mexico. The Oaxaca valley is noted for ethnic Mayan culture.

Memories with Mom - All mementos are not found abroad. When two sisters took their mother to Oaxaca, they received a wonderful note of thanks. The handwritten note is now part of the memory and is displayed in the keepsake album.

Photojournalism

In the midst of delivering worldly news and events to the American people, LIFE Magazine played a key role in the development of photo essays. LIFE assigned photographers to stories and many times there were no accompanying writers. The photographers knew more about the events than anyone else so by default photographers were also assigned to write the story, hence the title photojournalist. The written story was at the discretion of the photographer and the essay often resulted in a collection of photos arranged in sensible order with mere captions describing the newsworthy event.

Photojournalistic techniques of planning, editing and organizing transform photos into stories. Although a drawer full of snapshots is supply enough to arrange an essay, the opportunity for an anticipated picture shoot allows the photographer time to plan his shots in conjunction with the storyline.

Photographers take into consideration size, sequence, effect and purpose. They draft an outline pertaining to the theme and tone in order to arouse such feelings as inspiration, humor, anger or compassion. The sight, equipment, atmosphere, action, preparations and tools which lead up to the event or subject are all significant points of the narrative...a story with a beginning, a middle and an end.

To Camp El Tesoro

In San M[...]

Suzanne Browne was the oldest of three g[...]
Born in 1943, she grew up in Dallas, Texas [...]
loved horses and nature. Summertime w[...]
favorite. She spent two weeks at Camp El[...]
where they taught horseback riding, an[...]
weeks in Colorado for annual family [...]
another opportunity to ride. In high [...]
was a camp counselor in Estes Par[...]
Being big sister to Brendy and Am[...]
way into girlhood, school-age, [...]
college and eventually marriage [...]
Here lies a collection of childho[...]

Suzanne 9 years old, Nany, Amy, Brendy

Adorable at 2 years

Matching Summer Dresses

Junior High School picture

Easter 1944 - 14 Months

Off to school

Christmas Dance
Blaine
[...]mie

Girls in Grass Skirts - Summer

Wirn Sisters - Brendy & Amy

GOALS:
1. Get Married
2. Have 4 Children
3. Live Happily Ever A[...]

1957 MOTHER

Suzann[...]

LIFE: Get Married 2x - 6 C[...]

Archival Memories

To be remembered, not forgotten - My grandmother came across an old cigar box full of photos my Mom kept from high school. That box was the story of my Mom before she was a Mom. As I studied each photo, I wondered about her sisters, Brendy and Amy, about the boys she danced with and about her best friends. As her hair grew longer and she grew taller, the fashions changed.

I wanted to know more. Who were her friends? How, when and where did she meet the one who would be my Dad? Inquiring about the details brought stories. I savored every word as I met not Mom, but Suzanne for the very first time.

Her life was: Summer vacations to Colorado, where she explored mountains full of nature's charming delights, fresh streams where water could be sipped straight from glacier cold springs, horseback rides and hiking, a chair lift high above the hills, where she heard stories from Aunt Peggy, the outrageous and admired aunt.

The time spent learning about Mom inspired thoughts about my own life. The decisions she made guided her future and subsequently guided mine. I realized my fascination with her life was giving me clues about my own.

Born 1914
Dallas, TEXAS

Billy Browne

FORWARD FOR THE SUNDAY
SCHOOL CAGE CHAMPS AND AN
ALL-CITY MAN AT N. DALLAS HI
IN '31. HAS LEAD THE LEAGUE IN
SCORING FOR 2 CONSECUTIVE YEARS!!

BILLY IS ONE OF
THE MOST IMPROVED
CAGERS IN THE CITY
IN THE LAST COUPLE
OF YEARS!!

BEFORE
AND
AFTER

Joe Malony

Billy Browne
North Dallas H.S.

in Italy

S/SGT. WILLIAM G. BROWNE
"The Proud Father"
Dallas, Texas

1944

Billy,
Daddy
Browne
and
Aunt
Peggy.

Dallas, Texas. His family grew up in a drug
store. As a boy, his mother,
Baba, took him to Yellowstone
Park in a model-T Ford... they

Billy Browne

Gus Erwin

GUARD ON THE EAST DALLAS
CHRISTIAN CAGE TEAM, WAS ALL-
CITY CENTER AT FOREST HI, ALL-
AMERICAN ACADEMY FORWARD
AT TERRILL PREP AND ALL-STATE
SUNDAY SCHOOL GUARD!!

GUS IS A HOT SHOT
AT SINKING THE LONG
SHOT FROM THE
SIDES OF THE COURT

Billy Brow

FORWARD FOR THE
SCHOOL CAGE CHAN
ALL-CITY MAN AT
IN '31. HAS LEAD
SCORING FOR 2 CO

BILLY IS
THE MOT
CAGERS
THE LAST
OF YEAR

Lois and Billy Browne
MARRIED 1938

Bill worked
for the
telephone
company...
Southwestern
Bell yellow
pages.

WM. G. BROWNE
Directory Sales
Supervisor
NYPS

W.W.II - World War
II - Billy was
stationed in Italy
He trained as a
glider pilot.
camped out every nite and
their rabbit and canary and even took
trip. Billy made the 'list night touchdown'
in the Cottonbowl and was voted
'Most Popular Boy' in high
school.
Died 1981

Billy and
baby
Suzanne
1943.

Lois
and
Bill

Archival Preservation

What is harmful to photographs? *Magnetic page albums are hazardous to photos. They cause premature fading and discoloration of your photos. And there is no space to write. Self-adhesive backing often permanently attaches photos to the pages under dangerous plastic overlays which turn pages yellow or brown.*

Pocket Page albums made from PVC (polyvinyl chloride) can release gases that cause rapid deterioration. In a mere three to five years pictures can fade almost completely. PVC eats your pictures. For protective pockets made of plastic look for polyester, polyethylene, polypropylene and triacetate content.

Construction paper scrapbooks contain high acid content and accelerate the fading of photos. In addition, the paper itself will deteriorate with time and become too fragile to handle. Durable pages with a low acid content are conducive to protecting pictures and other mementos.

Cardboard boxes and shoe boxes give off gases and peroxides which tarnish and cause fading. Brown paper envelopes are made of a low-grade fiber and additives which cause fading. Ultraviolet light from bright sun causes fading and oxidation. High temperatures cause chemical changes, gritty dirt and dust from the air cause scratching, moisture and humidity cause fungus growth. Temperatures of 65-70°F with a relative humidity of approximately 40 percent are ideal.

Rubber cement is a harmful adhesive, try purchasing an archival glue which promotes longevity and permanence. Some adhesives and glues can cause discoloration or bleaching.

Albums & Photo Storage

In old black & white photos, people never smiled and yet everyone smiles for photos today. Somber expressions were not a sign of hard times, just a way to keep portraits from blurring. Before film was invented the image set on photographic plates and the subject had to be very still so the image would be clear. Smiling for minutes was difficult so people chose the most relaxed pose with the least expression.

How long you want to insure the image of your photo, is a consideration before starting your album. Photos can last for hundreds of years with special attention to materials, storage and conditions. Photography is a chemical process, and like all chemical processe, is subject to natural, ongoing deterioration.

Archival quality materials help preserve photographs. Archival means materials are acid-neutral or acid-free to ensure that acids will not eat away your photos. Professional conservators use materials that are 100% acid and lignin-free, PVC (polyvinyl chloride) free, durable, and lasting.

Photos are preserved best in a cool, dark and dry place free of dust and dirt. Store photos in the rooms where you live, not in hot attics or damp basements.

continued on page 94...

Norris & Freda Turner

· · · JULIE GAIL · · ·

1949   1975

Mother, Daughter

Daughter

Grand-Daughter

Remember Family & Friends

Times to Remember - Archival black and white photographs may be fragile to the touch in their old age. Quality copy centers are a good source for reproducing a number of photos inexpensively. You may feel more comfortable cropping reproductions of archivally valuable photographs.

Parents Wedding Day - Of all the family bonds, there is none so special as the bond between mother and daughter, only realized when a child is placed in your arms, just as with Julie's mom years before.

My Mother - Born in Spain while my grandfather was building a dam in the Pyranees Mountains, my mother still has snapshots from when she was a baby. To me these 80 year old photos are treasures.

Growing Up - My mother saved my birth certificate and photos of me as a baby, toddler and young girl. Rummaging through a box of old photos revealed an unlikely find. The photo of a young girl all dolled up and wearing a set of borrowed high heels. The photo matched another photo taken some 35 years later of that girl's daughter...identical down to the pose, hairdo and beautiful smile.

Uncle Duncan - With room to journal and write of the importance of this scarf, note and war portrait, a small album frames each memento.

My Family - I was an only child until I was 8 years old. These old photos of my family remind me of the happy times we had together.

Pearl Irene

Greene~
Broome~
Courbat

Born~
October 12, 1912
Doddridge, Arkansas

GRANDMA

Her love is
the kind
that will
always be
A part of
God's
beautiful
plan
To make you
feel
cherished
and special
and dear
As only a
grandmother
can

Grandma...
Your warm
and gentle kindness
is a blessing
in my life.

IT'S A BLESSING TO HAVE A GRANDMA LIKE YOU

Time Span Photos

Romancing the past - Archivalists are inspired to recreate the lifespan of an individual for history's sake. Families are inspired for the sentiments memories bring. A separate page for a mother and daughter from infancy to adulthood is commemorative. The story of these lives is the family history which was only committed in writing, perhaps a family tree inside the front cover of the family Bible.

Grandmother - Putting together a page of memories can be a real labor of love. Ancestors are influences in life and when they pass on, the memory is more important than the photographs.

Golden Girls - A collection of good friends is pictured here. The group of girls have been close from their teen years until now...in their 80's. The photos document changes and comeraderie.

Details Make a Difference - A picture in the newspaper is a special occurrence. After receiving an award from peers in the community, a photo was taken for the family album.

A Horse of Course - When Kristy was 6 years old, we took a family trip to Mexico City. In Chapultapec Park, she just had to have her photo taken on the wooden horse. At 16 she returned to Mexico and just had to have their photo taken on another wooden horse.

Growing Up - A record of family and childhood milestones will be a treasure forever... the first car, the first dance, Mom and Dad. Don't let valuable moments get away.

> "The best inheritance a mother and father can leave their children is good memories."

friends

STOP! Wait!
Read this INVITATION now,
BEFORE You Make a Ticket to HIA!

Friendship Journals

In the 19th century, Friendship Albums were common to young ladies and were exchanged among friends to gather sentiments of days past. Discovering the meaning and importance of friendship inspired them to share thoughts in poems, journal entries, cut paper, locks of hair, and drawings of flowers and nature.

Some were schoolgirl souvenir albums between students. Some were collections of thoughts and desires for which words were not to be spoken. Some were diaries of the hardships of travel or moving away from familiar friends, family and home.

In all, Victorian journals recorded the dearest moments of life, death, marriages, births, events of children, pleasures of the company of friends and thoughts from the heart.

Journaling can be many things. Shown on the following pages is a Friendship Memory Album I made to commemorate Mom's sort-of-annual Birthday & Slumber Party.

I collected photos and memorabilia for the album, then I asked that each person write or draw a creative page.

Lani

All Night Slumber Party Time

Several people brought cameras to the party and all shared copies of their photos to create this album. Arranging images from each roll provided a wide assortment of color, subject and interest.

The pages that fill the Slumber Party & Birthday Party album are treasures. Each page was created by a friend. At the Slumber Party, an inexpensive artist sketch book of blank white paper was left open to encourage guests to write or draw a remembrance for the Friendship Album.

Whimsical pictures drawn in bold markers accent an oval picture in a double mat. A banner across two pages leaves ample space for a bold title and a journal style summary to be filled in.

Mary's note refers to her love of lace. A paper doily imitates a dainty lace design. By slowly turning the page as you write, a circle is formed.

A fun page features a few segments from the party invitation, a map, a photo and a cartoon.

A simple black and white sketch of the New York City skyline is joined by a photo of Julia. Renee drew a Georgia peach as a symbol of the distance she traveled to join the celebration. An 'All Night, All Day' collage of photos captures candid poses.

Sunflowers are picture perfect shapes for round photos. A greeting card inspired the topiary design which was tinted with rubber stamp markers. Other party-goers sketched with festive colors.

Archival Photos

Photos in antique albums may still be in good condition but more times than not the black paper pages are crumbling with deterioration from time. It is time to carefully remove the photos and transfer them to a new album with archival quality pages.

More recent acid albums may endanger the image and color of pictures. Plastic sleeves containing PVC and magnetic albums can cause fading and yellowing. Besides lacking archival quality care for the images, limited room for writing descriptions results in a loss of historical importance. Without thought and planning, a haphazard arrangement of photos portrays a confusing story and leaves many questions unanswered. Preserving the stories, the memories, the photos and all the clues to life make albums treasures for generations to come.

The life expectancy of color pictures is limited. Because color photos are formed from dyes and with time all dyes fade, a few black and white photos included in any collection of family archives is helpful. A yearly permanent record of black and white photos is recommended by archivalists. Just take the basics...each person in the family, the dog, cat, a picture of your house or car. After ten years this collection becomes a priceless treasure.

Negatives - Store negatives separately from albums. If a freak disaster happens to your albums such as a fire, theft or flood, your negatives will be safe. Negatives are irreplaceable.

A soft lead pencil is the best tool for writing on the back of photos. Avoid using ball-point pens because the ink will eventually bleed through to the front ruining the image.

For easy retrieval of negatives or photos, sort, index and label them with archival materials. Photo storage boxes stack compactly on shelves and can be labeled to identify contents. Better made boxes are constructed of heavy-duty acid-free paper and are secured with metal clips, without adhesives that can cause discoloration or bleaching. The boxes come in different sizes, but should be packed full when stored so the prints will not curl.

Use acid-free envelopes and negative sleeves to organize and label each roll of film. A date, theme and comments are enough to remind you of what is inside of each envelope. Secure envelopes snugly in archival quality negative boxes.

Growing Up

One picture brings to mind an entire story, memories to be saved and shared.

In this photo, I immediately recognized the four of us as young children, Kristy, Kelley, Steven and me, in bathing suits showing off an enormous stingray we discovered on the beach. Every summer the family vacation destination was Corpus Christi, an eight hour drive to the coast from Dallas-Fort Worth. Far away but never to be forgotten. The photograph brings back memories of:

Mother's infamous packing list ~ one small bag with bathing suit, three shirts, two shorts and sneakers.

Our typical menu ~ peanut butter, jelly and banana sandwiches for lunch and spaghetti for dinner, every night.

A family tradition ~ one trip to Dairy Queen for the ice cream of choice and one trip to Port Aransas for a shirt with anything on it but most importantly with the insignia of the shop name, Pat Magee's, so that everyone back home would know you had really been.

Souvenirs, shells, sand dollars, starfish and sand, which seemed to accumulate in every crevice.

Lani Stiles, age 11

*"Families and friends...
memories of love without end."*

We Crop Until We Drop

Every Thursday night we get together at Julie's house. She has a big dining room table for us to spread out supplies. Our mission is to share stories, choose photos, tell stories, eat, arrange pages, listen to stories, cut, punch and glue.

We have become the best of friends as we laugh, giggle, cry, share creative ideas, admire each page, and paste pages for personal Family Memory Albums. When we return home, often after midnight, we take home pages filled with priceless records of family and friends.

We had so much fun creating the sample pages that fill this book, and we can't wait for an excuse to start organizing pages for last year, next year and the year after that. We hope this book will inspire you to create a priceless Family Memory Album for your children.

Ideas Sparklers *- Fill your pages with designs for holidays, celebrations, school and camp. Bring a touch of imagination to every page. Remember the look on Amy's face at the surprise party? What was the theme...Pink...Blue...Teddy Bears? Who collected the most watermelon seeds? What did you get for Christmas?*

Fun Questions - *You'll be amazed what you find out about people. Try some of these fun questions. In what way are you and your brothers or sisters alike? What is a question you'd like to ask your grandparents? What is your favorite childhood memory? How did your parents meet? What is a question you'd like to ask your parents? How are your father and grandfather alike? What is your favorite saying? What is your favorite sport? How are you like your mother? How are you like your father? How are your mother and grandmother alike? What was your favorite meal when you were a kid? What did you do on Sundays as a kid? What do you do now?*

Descriptions - *Describe something you like about your brother or sister. Describe something your mother or father considers very important. Describe something you did with your brother or sister. Describe your best and worst teachers. Describe something you like to do for fun. Describe your first date. Describe something you did with your family. Name and describe someone you admire. Describe something that your father enjoyed. Describe one of the oldest photographs you have. Describe your first experience living away from home. Describe an event you'll never forget from school. Describe your mother. Describe your father. Describe your best friend.*

Tell a Story - *Tell about a famous person you have met. Tell about a favorite card you received. Tell a story about your aunt. Tell a story about your uncle. Tell about your first dance. Tell about your dinner time. Tell about your favorite Birthday. Tell about your favorite smell. Retell about a time you got in trouble at school.*

Preserving Family Memories for your children and grandchildren is fun and important. We know you'll love albums as much as we do. Don't wait another minute, start planning today.

Linda, Virginia, Suzanne, Jean, Delores, Barbara, Donna, Julie & Kim

Family Memories

Growing up I always wondered about my grandmother's childhood. Who were her close friends? What did they do together? What was her mother like? So many unanswered questions and really no way to know except for the hints and the few stories she has been able to share.

'Mom' has always been a role model because of her strength, her ingenuity and her care. We don't have to look far for some of the most important teachers of life. She taught me how to make the tallest, lightest, most spectacular melt in your mouth meringue there ever was. I'll never forget the day we made it together. Mile High Meringue contained all her secrets. Gently break up the egg whites and turn on the mixer to low. Add the sugar little by little all the while watching for high peaks of white smooth cloudlike forms to appear. Next choose a favorite filling to top ... chocolate, coconut, or lemon ... ooh la la. Bake until just golden and delectable. The hardest part came next. Cool on a rack for three whole hours until all the flavors set. Every pie ever made by 'Mom's' wonderful hands was praised for years to come. And now I too hold the secrets of her magic. It wasn't only the meringue, it was the warm hands and warm heart that she baked into every motion and word. She was giving me part of herself and part of our heritage on that day long ago.

I came to realize that it wasn't her past and her mother's past which was important, it was learning about my grandmother with my grandmother that was important. I found out that I was actually learning something about myself and my heritage.

Photo Templates - Photocopy the template shapes. Position a photo over the shape then trace over a 'light table'. Cut out the photo. Note: Shapes may be enlarged or reduced.

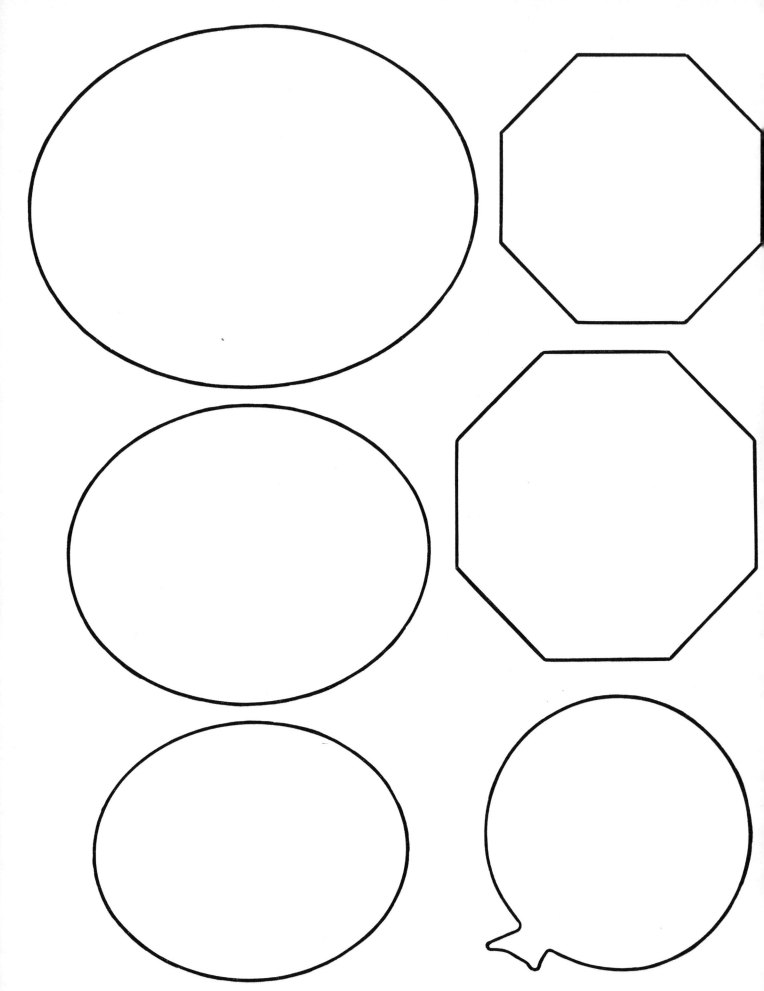

Photo Templates - Photocopy the template
shapes. Position a photo over the shape then
trace over a 'light table'. Cut out the photo.
Note: Shapes may be enlarged or reduced.

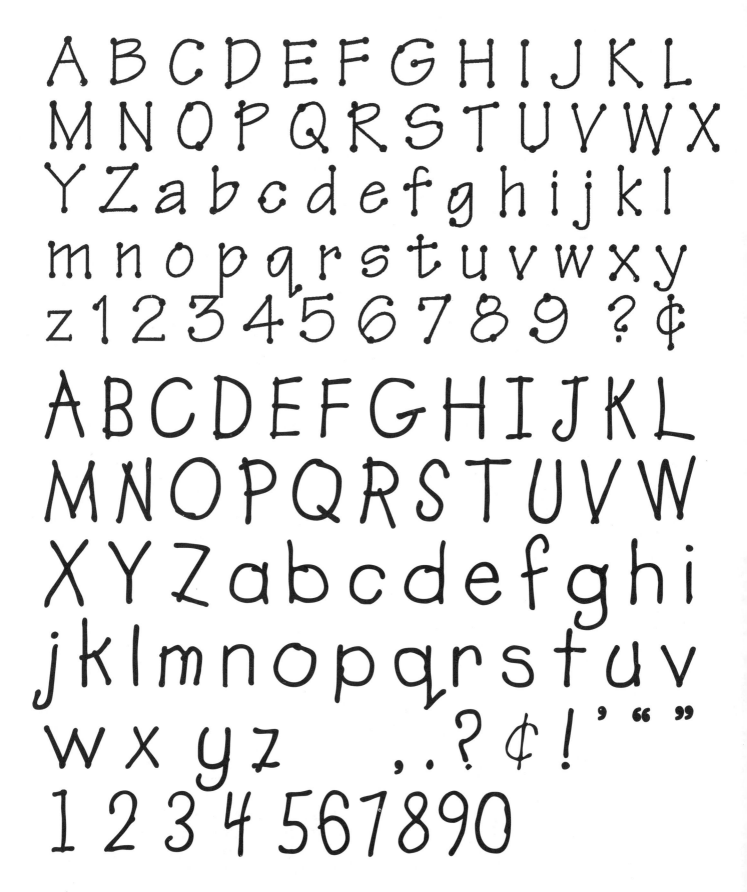

ABCDEFGHIJKL
MNOPQRSTUVWX
YZabcdefghijkl
mnopqrstuvwxy
z123456789?¢

ABCDEFGHIJKL
MNOPQRSTUVW
XYZabcdefghi
jklmnopqrstuv
wxyz ,.?¢!'""
1234567890

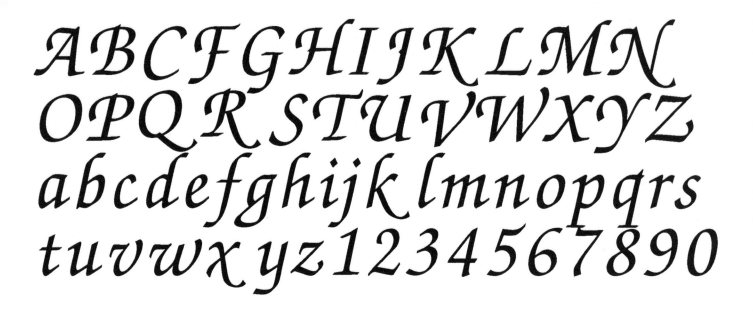

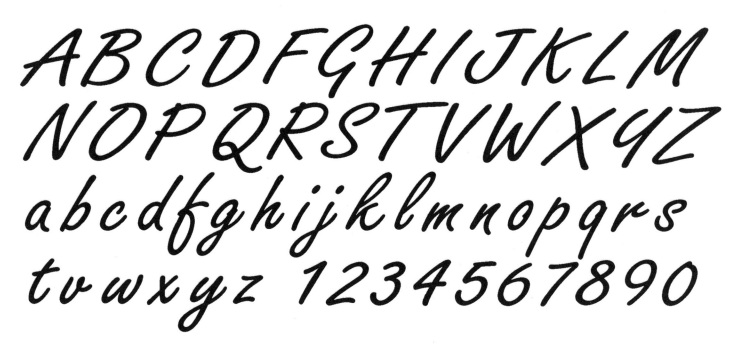

ABCDEFGHIJKLMN
OPQRSTUVWYZab
cdefghijklmnopqrs
tuvwxyz1234567890

ABCDEFGHIJKLM
NOPQRSTVWXYZ
abcdefghijklmnopq
rstvwxyz1234567890

ABCDEFGHIJK
LMNOPQRSTUV
WXYZabcdefgh
ijklmnopqrstuv
wxyz1234567890

ABCDEFGHIJKL
MNOPQRSTUVW
XYZabcdefghijklmnop
qrstvwxyz1234567890

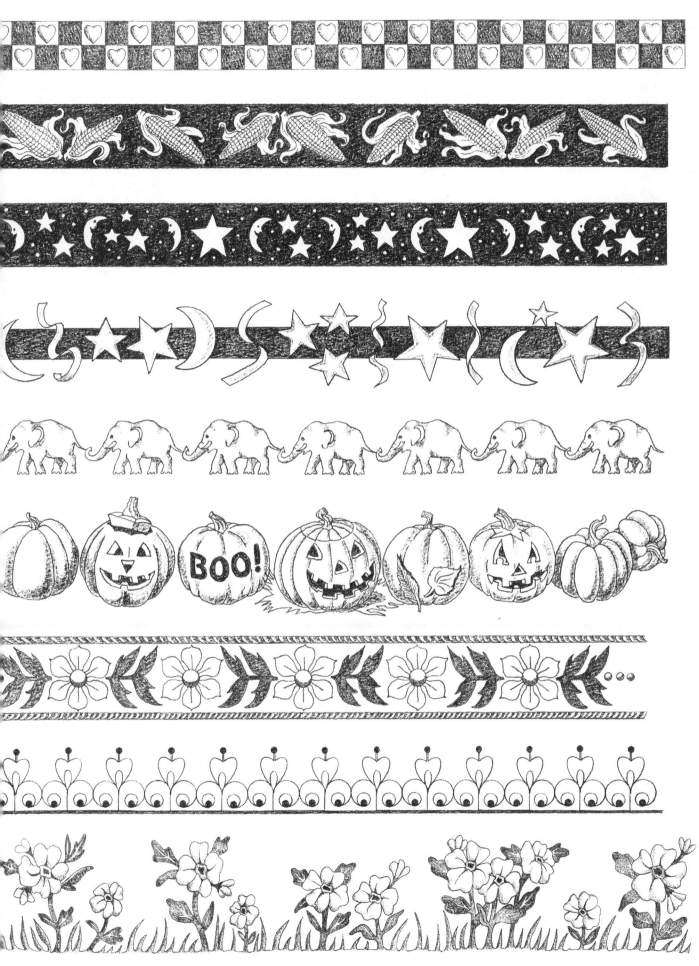

AND THE TWO SHALL BE AS ONE

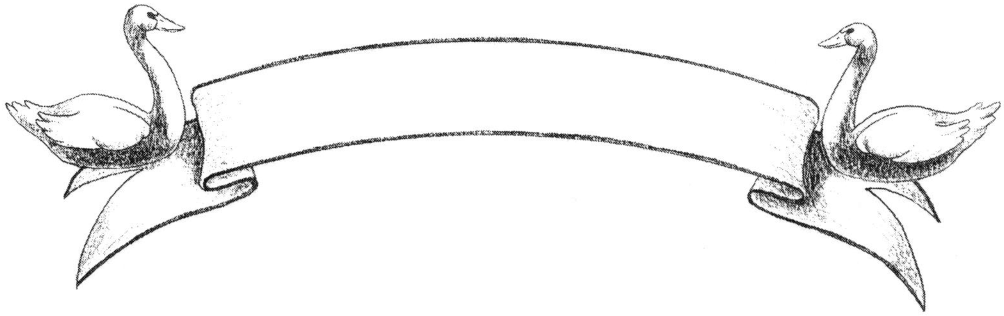

Life is Full of Angels

Clip Art Motifs - Photocopy your
favorite design. Color the design with
colored pencils then cut around it with
tiny scissors or an X-acto® craft knife
and mat. Finally glue the design on
your album page.
Note: Designs may be enlarged or reduced.

Clip Art Motifs - Photocopy your favorite design. Color the design with colored pencils then cut around it with tiny scissors or an X-acto® craft knife and mat. Finally glue the design on your album page. Note: Designs may be enlarged or reduced on a photocopy machine.

HOLIDAY

Spring

Autumn

Winter

Summer

FUN AND

Design pictured on page 70.
Note: Designs may be enlarged or reduced on a photocopy machine.

Design pictured on pages 44-45.
Note: Designs may be enlarged or reduced on a photocopy machine.

Design pictured on page 56.
Note: Designs may be enlarged or reduced on a photocopy machine.

Design pictured on pages 52-53.
Note: Designs may be enlarged or reduced on a photocopy machine.

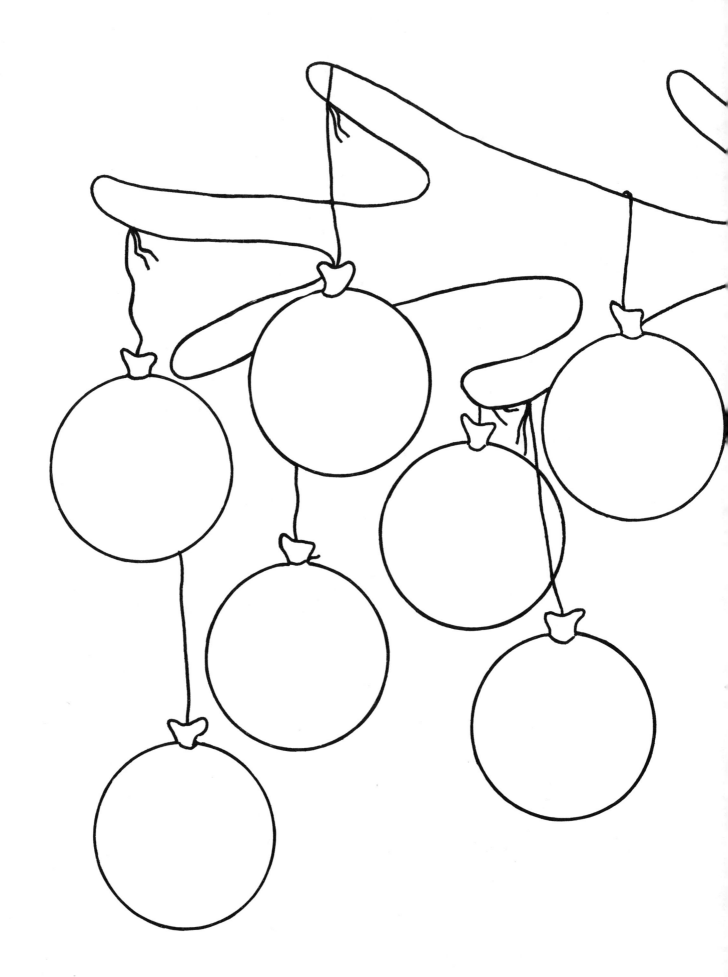

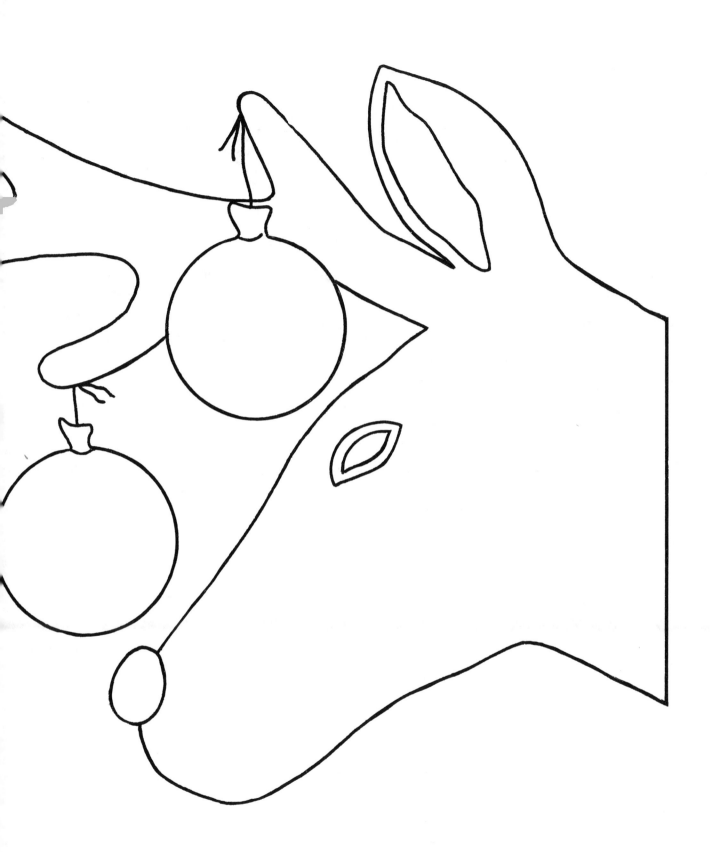

Design pictured on page 55.
Note: Designs may be enlarged or reduced on a photocopy machine.

Let Us Hear from You

We hope you have enjoyed viewing and hearing all the good things about our friends and family. We believe that these pages will inspire you to begin remembering valuable memories with your loved ones. It has been fun sharing with you, my friend. It is a treat to receive notes from each of you and we would love to answer every bit of correspondence. Every encouraging and kind letter is filed for safe keeping.

When we read stories about how photos, albums and journals have filled a void in someone's life, we know **Family Memories** are what we want to be pursuing. Photo albums and journals bring happiness to friends and family. They provide comfort to loved ones, inspire others to feel good about themselves, and make children smile with pride.

We invite you to share your special moments, photos and stories in our next Memory Albums book. Please write for details (enclose a self-addressed stamped envelope) to Suzanne & Lani, **Design Originals**, 2425 Cullen Street, Fort Worth, TX 76107.

Suzanne & Lani

Design pictured on pages 68-69.
Note: Designs may be enlarged or reduced on a photocopy machine.

Memories

Family ***Memories*** *is a very special collection containing the creativity of many people. Each album page takes on the ingenuity and indivudual style of its maker. No two people work in exactly the same way, and that individuality is what makes each page unique. Working on this book has been a celebration of friends and family...a guide to remember events which evoke the taking of photos and the memories that are alive within each of us.*

Photos

Over the course *of the last five years, Americans have taken part in a photographic frenzy capturing their most precious moments on film. With sixty-four million families taking four billion snapshots per year, photo albums and journals are an awaiting opportunity.*

Thank You

Special thanks *to family and friends who shared special moments, feelings, time and photographs for the collection of memories in this book. There wouldn't be a book without these special friends, Barbara Burnett, Jean & Laura Kievlan, Julie McGuffee, Linda Rocamontes, Virginia Tucker, Kim Ballor, Delores Frantz, Todd Stiles and Kristy McNeill.*

To David and Donna Thomason for the care they took to create the most beautiful photographs.

Love to our family and friends for posing for photographs.

SOURCES

Many photo, craft, card and art supply stores carry an excellent assortment of supplies for Memory Albums. If you need something special ask your local store to contact the following companies.

Supplies & Albums

LIGHT IMPRESSIONS
Archival Supplies
439 Monroe Avenue
P.O. Box 940
Rochester, NY 14603
1-800-828-6216   catalog

EXPOSURES
1 Memory Lane
P.O. Box 3615
Oshkosh, WI 54903
1-800-572-5750   catalog

Decorative Supplies

FAMILY TREASURES
Templates, Scissors, Punches Rulers, Stencils and more!
14540 S.W. 136th St. - Ste 106
Miami, FL 33186

Photo Albums

Antioch WEBWAY
Archival Acid-Free Albums
P.O. Box 767
St. Cloud, MN 56302

CACHET
Acid-Free Spiral Albums
300 Fairfield R.
Fairfield, NJ 07004

C.R. GIBSON
32 Knight
Norwalk, CT 06856

KODAK
343 State Street
Rochester, NY 14650

PIONEER
9801 Deering Avenue
Chatsworth, CA 91311

Mini-Trimmer & Xacto®

HUNT
Mini-Trimmer, Knife, Mat & Markers
2301 Speedball Way
Statesville, NC 28687

Deckle Rulers

DESIGN A CARD
P.O. Box 5314
Englewood, FL 34224

Markers

E.K. SUCCESS
Calligraphy & Brush Markers
611 Industrial Road
Carlstadt, NJ 07072

SAKURA
Pigma® Pens & Markers
19800 Hawthorne Bld. #218
Torrance, CA 90503

Scissors & Punches

FISKARS
Wavy edge Wcissors & Punches
7811 West Stewart Avenue
Wausau, WI 54401

UCHIDA OF AMERICA
LePlume Brush Markers & Punches
CA3535 Del Amo Blvd.
Torrance, CA 90503

Mini Light Tables

AMER. TRADITIONAL STENCILS
Route 4, Box 317A
Northwood, NH 03261

Mini Light Table
ME SEW Inc.
Valencia, CA

Tape & Glue

3M - SCOTCH
3M Bldg. 221 - 5N - 38
De Paul, MN 55144

LIQUID PAPER
Box 621 - Gillette
Boston, MA 02199

Colored Papers

CANSON: *Acid-Free papers*
21 Industrial Drive
S. Hadley, MA 01085

KATE'S PAPERIE
561 Broadway
New York, NY 10012
1-800-809-9880   catalog

PAPER ACCESS
23 West 18th Street
New York, NY 10011
1-212-463-7035   catalog

Decorative Stickers

UNIEK: *Photo Humor*
805 Uniek Dr - P.O.Box 457
Waunekee, WI 53597

MRS. GROSSMAN'S: *Acid-Free*
3810 Cypress Drive
Petaluma, CA 94954

SANDYLION
P.O. Box 1570
Buffalo, NY 14240

SUZY'S ZOO
9401 Waples Street, S. 150
San Diego, CA 92121

THE GIFTED LINE
99 Canal Blvd.
Point Richmon, CA 94804

Rubber Stamps

GRAPHIC RUBBER STAMP
11250 Magnolia Blvd.
No. Hollywood, CA 91601

HAMPTON ART STAMPS
19 Industrial Blvd.
Medford, NY 11763

HERO ARTS
1343 Powell Street
Emeryville, CA 94608

INKADINKADO
60 Cummings Park
Woburn, MA 01801

RUBBER STAMPEDE
P.O. Box 246
Berkeley, CA 94701

STAMPENDOUS Inc.
1357 South Lewis Street
Anaheim, CA 92805

Templates & Stencils

GICK
9 Studebaker Drive
Irvine, CA 92718

PLAID
1649 International Court
Norcross, GA 30091

STENCIL HOUSE
410 Wentworth No.
Hamilton, Ontario,
CANADA L8L5W3

Family Memories

Each family has its own traditions and memories. Every box of precious photographs and different set of valuable memories is as familiar a vision to us as our own childhood.

In this stunning volume, Suzanne McNeill and Lani Stiles describe the inspiration behind each album page and give advice on how to implement your own family's memories and photos to produce very personal pages.

This valuable book presents a collection of memorable themes...baby, wedding, school, family, travel and archival. Inspiring ideas and dozens of album pages that you, your family and your friends can enjoy together are all here. It is a valuable companion for anyone wanting to save photographs and life's stories for generations to come.

Family Memories captures the mood, the memories, and the magic of our most cherished moments.

To order additional **Family Memories** copies:
#5005 Soft cover book, 128 pages..........$21.99
#3172 Memory Albums starter book, 12 pages....$ 6.99
    Postage and handling, per order...... ...$ 4.00
Quantity Discounts Available

I enclose $_____. Please send check, money order, or charge to VISA / Mastercard. Make check payable to **Design Originals** and mail to 2425 Cullen St, Fort Worth, TX 76107.

for easy ordering
Call 1-800-877-7820
or FAX 1-817-877-0861

Phone (_____) -_____

Name _____

Address _____

City-State-Zip _____
Prices and availability are subject to change without notice.

Suzanne McNeill is the founder of **Design Originals**, a highly successful craft book publishing company with over 400 'how-to' titles to date. Creative vision has placed her books on top of the trends for over 20 years.

With the ability to recognize popular concepts and the talent to display good ideas, **Design Originals** books are always in demand. In this remarkable book Suzanne and her daughter Lani, team up to create a beautiful sourcebook of lasting value for any family.

We invite you and your loved ones to share cherished photos, **Family Memories** and all the magical moments that will be treasured for years to come.

Credits
Creative Art Director ♥ Patty Cox
Art Director ♥ Janet Long
Managing Editor ♥ Kathy McMillan
Artists ♥ Teresa Plum & Carol VanNess
Editors ♥ Wanda Little & Colleen Reigh